The Pedagogy of the Open Society

Open Education
Volume 01

Series Editors
Michael A. Peters,
Professor Emeritus, *University of Illinois at Urbana-Champaign, USA*
Professor, Policy, Cultural & Social Studies in Education, *University of Waikato, Hamilton, New Zealand*

Editorial Board:
Tina Besley, *University of Waikato, NZ*
Ourania Filippakou, *London Institute of Education*
Gareth Williams, *London Institute of Education*
James Reveley, *University of Wollongong, Australia*
Peter Roberts, *University of Canterbury, NZ*
Jayne White, *University of Waikato, NZ*
Wang Chengbing, *Beijing Normal University*
Ruyu Hung, *National Chiayi University, Taiwan*
Simon Marginson, *Melbourne University*

Scope
"Open education involves a commitment to openness and is therefore inevitably a political and social project. The concept of openness in regard to education pre-dates the openness movement that begins with free software and open source in the mid 1980s with roots going back to the Enlightenment that are bound up with the philosophical foundations of modern education with its commitments to freedom, citizenship, knowledge for all, social progress and individual transformation. Yet in another way political, social and technological developments have taken place in parallel alongside the history of the movement of open education that have heightened certain political and epistemological features and technological enabled others that emphasize questions of access to knowledge, the co-production and co-design of educational programs and of knowledge, the sharing, use, reuse and modification of resources while enhancing the ethics of participation and collaboration. Open education as a movement sits within the broader framework of the history of openness that brings together a number of disciplines and fields to impact directly upon the value of knowledge and learning, their geographic distribution and ownership, and their organization."
http://www.ffst.hr/ENCYCLOPAEDIA/doku.php?id=open_education_and_educati on_for_openness

This new series is devoted to the general theory and practice of open education in all its forms.

The Pedagogy of the Open Society

Knowledge and the Governance of Higher Education

Michael A. Peters
University of Waikato, Hamilton, New Zealand

Tze-Chang Liu
Graduate Institute of Education, Tunghai University, Taiwan

and

David J. Ondercin
University of Illinois, Champaign, USA

SENSE PUBLISHERS
ROTTERDAM/BOSTON/TAIPEI

A C.I.P. record for this book is available from the Library of Congress.

ISBN: 978-94-6091-965-7 (paperback)
ISBN: 978-94-6091-966-4 (hardback)
ISBN: 978-94-6091-967-1 (e-book)

Published by: Sense Publishers,
P.O. Box 21858,
3001 AW Rotterdam,
The Netherlands
https://www.sensepublishers.com/

Printed on acid-free paper

TABLE OF CONTENTS

RADICAL OPENNESS: A POLITICAL THEORY OF SOCIAL INSTITUTIONS

Institutions are the rules of the game in a society or, more formally, are the humanly devised constraints that shape human interaction.

–Douglass C. North (1990) *Institutions, Institutional Change and Economic Performance*, p. 3

This was our paradox: no course of action could be determined by a rule, because every course of action can be made out to accord with the rule. the answer was: if everything can be made out to accord with the rule, then it can also be made out to conflict with it. and so there would be neither accord nor conflict here.

It can be seen that there is a misunderstanding here from the mere fact that in the course of our argument we give one interpretation after another; as if each one contented us at least for a moment, until we thought of yet another standing behind it. What this shews is that there is a ways of grasping a rule which is *not* an *interpretation*, but which is exhibited in what we call "obeying the rule" and "going against it" in actual cases.

–Ludwig Wittgenstein, (1953) *Philosophical Investigations*, §201

INTRODUCTION

Openness is a complex code word that represents a change of philosophy and ethos, a set of interrelated and complex changes that transforms markets, the mode of production and consumption, ushering in a new collection of values based on *openness*, the ethic of participation and peer-to-peer collaboration. These changes indicate a broader shift from an underlying metaphysics of production—a 'productionist' metaphysics—to a metaphysics of consumption as use, reuse and modification with new logics and different patterns of cultural consumption in the areas of new media where symbolic analysis becomes a habitual and daily creative activity. The new language of 'prosuming' and 'produsage' is an attempt to capture open participation, communal evaluation, fluid heterarchy and equipotentiality, common property with individual rewards (Bruns, 2008). Information is the vital element in a 'new' politics and economy that links space, knowledge and capital in networked practices. Freedom is an essential ingredient in this equation if these network practices develop or transform themselves into knowledge cultures.

Social processes and policies that foster *openness* as an overriding value as evidenced in the growth of open source, open access and open education and their convergences that characterize global knowledge communities that transcend borders of the nation-state. Openness seems also to suggest political transparency and the norms of open inquiry, indeed, even democracy itself as both the basis of the logic of inquiry and the dissemination of its results.

These changes and insights have been the basis for a series of major reports by the U.S. Committee for Economic Development with its most recent report on Open Standards, Open Source, and Open Innovation: Harnessing the Benefits of Openness (Maxwell, April 2006) that focuses on new collaborative models of 'open innovation,' originating outside the firm, that results in an 'architecture of participation.' Three major reports were published in the last few years: Giving Knowledge for Free: The Emergence Of Open Educational Resources (OECD, 2007); Open Educational Practices and Resources (OLCOS, 2007); A Review of the Open Educational Resources (OER) Movement: Achievements, Challenges, and New Opportunities (Atkins, Brown, & Hammond, 2007). As the OECD report puts it:

> An apparently extraordinary trend is emerging. Although learning resources are often considered as key intellectual property in a competitive higher education world, more and more institutions and individuals are sharing digital learning resources over the Internet openly and without cost, as open educational resources (OER) (OECD, 2007, p. 9).

Openness in education has a history that comprises a set of interrelated movements: The Open Classroom; Open Schooling; The Open University (UK); Open Courseware; Open Educational Resources (OER); Open Education. MIT OpenCourseWare has reached 35 million people and another 14 million in translation. The OpenCourseWare Consortium 'is a collaboration of more than 100 higher education institutions and associated organizations from around the world creating a broad and deep body of open educational content using a shared model.'

Open Education embodies three main aspects: openness of learning content (full courses, courseware, journals); tools for openness (software to support the development, use, reuse and delivery of learning content and management systems); implementation of openness (through IP licences to promote open publishing and design principles of best practice with localized content) (OECD, 2007). The Ithaka Report, *University Publishing In A Digital Age* (Brown, Griffiths, Rascoff, 2007) focuses on:

- *changes in creation, production and consumption of scholarly resources* – 'creation of new formats made possible by digital technologies, ultimately allowing scholars to work in deeply integrated electronic research and publishing environments that will enable real-time dissemination, collaboration, dynamically-updated content, and usage of new media' (p. 4), and,
- *'alternative distribution models* (institutional repositories, pre-print servers, open access journals) have also arisen with the aim to broaden access, reduce costs, and enable open sharing of content' (p. 4)

The recent Cape Town Open Education Declaration indicated that we are on the cusp of a global revolution in teaching and learning where educators worldwide are developing a vast pool of educational resources on the Internet, open and free for all to use.[1] *Open Education* builds on the nested and evolving convergences of open source, open access and open science, and also emblematic of a set of still wider political and economic changes that ushers in 'social production' as an aspect of the global digital economy (see Peters & Britez, 2008).

In *The Wealth of Networks: How Social Production Transforms Markets and Freedom* Benkler (2006) develops a vision of the good society based on access and distribution of information goods in a networked global information economy that places a high value on individual autonomy where within the public information space of the Internet and the information commons people have the individual means to pursue their own interests. The emergence of the global networked information economy made possible by increasingly cheaper processors linked as a pervasive network has created an information economy based on the production of information and culture that enables social and nonmarket or peer-to peer production and exchange to play a, perhaps even, the central role. Benkler's (2006) *The Wealth of Networks* links to a broader tradition of thought who have attempted to retheorize the public domain such as Jane Jacobs, James Scott, Richard Sennett and Iris Marion Young.

Openness is a value and philosophy that also offers us a means for transforming our institutions. Institutions are humanly devised; they set constraints and shape incentives. For example, economic institutions such as property rights, or contract shape economic incentives, contracting possibilities and distribution. Political institutions, including form of government, separation of powers and so on shape political incentives and distribution of political power. There is an important distinction to be made between formal institutions based on codified rules—such as a constitution—and informal institutions related to the question of the distribution of power, social norms, and equilibrium. Sociologists use the term 'institutions' to refer to complex social forms – including governments, the family, human languages, universities, hospitals, business corporations, and legal systems—that comprise

> a complex of positions, roles, norms and values lodged in particular types of social structures and organising relatively stable patterns of human activity with respect to fundamental problems in producing life-sustaining resources, in reproducing individuals, and in sustaining viable societal structures within a given environment, (Turner 1997: 6).

Clearly, "social institutions need to be distinguished from less complex social forms such as conventions, rules, social norms, roles and rituals" which "are among the constitutive elements of institutions" and from "more complex and more complete social entities, such as societies or cultures, of which any given institution is typically a constitutive element" (Miller, 2011). As Semus Miller (2011) goes on to argue "Social institutions are often organisations," and sometimes *systems* of organisations, and *meta-institutions* that organise other institutions—"thus governments regulate and coordinate economic systems, educational institutions, police and military organisations and so on largely by way of (enforceable) legislation."

He proceeds to give an account of social institutions within the scope of liberal democracy based on Rawls' (1972, 1999) account of distributive justice. It is perhaps surprising that he draws the distinction between economic and social institutions so exclusively. In the social sciences two broad types of institutions are advanced, both essentially political, although they exhibit different variations. The first that is the characteristic approach of neoclassical economics focuses on the behavior of the rational individual agent (so-called "rational utility maximisers") and treats all macrostates as simply the outcomes of interactions among individuals. The traditional ruling assumptions of this approach are associated with the revival of *homo economicus* based on individuality, rationality, and self-interest.

The alternative approach starts with social structures embedded in a historical context and views the individual as a reflection of or bearer of structures. In economic theory, this is a "agentless" view that emphasizes the governing effects of larger structures such as "culture," "society," and "economic system" that are comprised of organization and institutions. This kind of theory is characteristic of Marxian, radical, and institutionalist theories.

THE REASSERTION OF INSTITUTIONAL THEORIES

By the end of 1990s commentators were heralding the end of public choice and new public management with a resurgence of institutional theories based on March and Olsen (1984) famous paper. B. Guy Peters (2000: p. 1) writes:

> The past decade and a half have seen a major reassertion of institutional theories in the social sciences, and especially in political science. The March and Olsen (1984) article in the APSR was the beginning of the revolution against the methodological individualism of both behavioralism and rational choice approaches. Following from that and their subsequent publications (1989; 1994; Brunsson and Olsen, 1993; Olsen and Peters, 1996) there has been a proliferation of institutional theories and applications of those theories. Similarly, in economics (North, 1990; Alston, Eggerston and North, 1996; Khalil, 1995) and in sociology (DiMaggio and Powell, 1991; Scott, 1995; Zucker, 1987) there has been a birth (or more appropriately a resurrection) of institutional approaches to the basic questions in these disciplines.

Douglass North (1991: 97) is a stunning example of an economic approach to institutional theory that focuses on his earlier work relating to economic and institutional change. He writes

> Institutions are the humanly devised constraints that structure political, economic and social interaction. They consist of both informal constraints (sanctions, taboos, customs, traditions, and codes of conduct), and formal rules (constitutions, laws, property rights). Throughout history, institutions have been devised by human beings to create order and reduce uncertainty in exchange. Together with the standard constraints of economics they define the choice set and therefore determine transaction and production costs and hence the profitability and feasibility of engaging in economic activity. They

evolve incrementally, connecting the past with the present and the future; history in consequence is largely a story of institutional evolution in which the historical performance of economies can only be understood as a part of a sequential story. Institutions provide the incentive structure of an economy; as that structure evolves, it shapes the direction of economic change towards growth, stagnation, or decline.

Constraints, as North describes, are devised as formal rules (constitutions, laws, property rights) and informal restraints (sanctions, taboos, customs, traditions, code of conduct), which usually contribute to the perpetuation of order and safety within a market or society. The degree to which they are effective is subject to varying circumstances, such as a government's limited coercive force, a lack of organized state, or the presence of strong religious precept.

In 1997 he helped found the International Society for the New Institutional Economics that attempts to extend economics by focusing on the social and legal norms and rules that underlie economic activity. In the 1960s and after the rise of rational and public choice theories accompanied a revival of neoclassical economics based on *homo economicus* especially by the third generation Chicago school including Milton Friedman, Gary Becker and a number of other Nobel prize winners which swept everything before it and systematically replaced Keynesianism as the ruling orthodoxy (see Chapter 7).

While the economic theorists have been developing the new institutionalism governed by economic norms and principles applied the opeartions of social institutions, other social and political theorist have systematically critiqued the nature of closed institutions on the grounds that closed institutions typical of industrial modernity tend to be very manipulative and controlling.

DISCIPLINARY SOCIETIES, MANIPULATIVE INSTITUTIONS: FOUCAULT, ILLICH AND THE CRITIQUE OF WESTERN MODERNITY

There are broad similarities between the oeuvres of Michel Foucault and Ivan Illich and a set of overlapping interests even if there are differences in background, personal histories and philosophical approaches. These similarities and differences are useful points of reference as the similarities endorse one another and set up a deeper critique of the institutions of Western modernity than would be otherwise possible. Both Illich and Foucault were bought up as Catholics and develop a sense of history strongly featuring the influence of Christianity and the Church's shaping of institutions and subjectivities, even although their methods differ. Both employ broad historical approaches to the critique of Western modernity and its institutions and both take cybernetics as the starting point for a theory of institutions within a new type of emerging postmodern society characterized by closely articulated and interrelated systems.

One of the strongest parallels and sources of motivation for the work and for the similarities between them springs from the set of arguments associated with the anti-psychiatry movement that took root in the 1960s and '70s and developed as a fully fledged philosophy of deinstitutionalization guiding the process of reform of the large asylums. For Foucault, the analysis was in part an analysis of the history of subjectivity, of subject populations, in the early modern era. He was interested in marginalized groups and the forms of institutional enclosure of the prison, the school, and the clinic, and the production of "docile bodies". Foucault (1977; 1980) analyzed and described the process of institutional incarceration and its power/knowledge effects—the emergence of new discourses based on the gaze and surveillance of institutionalizaed individuals. For Illich, motivated by similar questions concerning freedom and its institutionalized forms, focuses on questions concerning the debilitating psychological and political effects of processes of institutionalization that he investigates in relation to what he calls "manipulative institutions" as opposed to what he calls "convivial institutions" that are characterized by spontaneous use. Illich also generalizes his critique to a critique of Western institutions aimed at growth and based on processes of consumption. He investigates a variety of different institutions, most famously the school, but also the hospital, and "disabling professions" associated with those institutions that have a compassionate image but paradoxically only produced more people who are psychologically dependent and have been robbed of the intellectual vitality. Illich, strongly influenced by his Jesuit past, worked with cultural minorities and understood that institutionalization was also one of the dominant processes of Western colonization.

There is nothing in the literature that compares these two important thinkers. We would encourage our readers to explore the parallels in their thinking in order to develop, strengthen and broaden their critique of Western modernity through the critique of institutions. What are the different forms of analysis that Illich and Foucault bring to bear on Western institutions, their subjectivity effects, their relationship to forms of governance, and a philosophy of deinstitutionalization? The experience of deinstitutionalization is a philosophy with a very complex policy history. Illich and Foucault are very important in the movement of anti-psychiatry that aims at altering the set of power relations within large asylums and institutions for mentally ill through the processes of deinstitutionalization. Both Illich and Foucault discuss forms of deinstitutionalization. Illich's move to "convivial institutions" is a philosophical basis for the improvement in the design of Western institutions and is remarkably foresightful in understanding the politics of the open institution based on the user—not user-pays but user-created. Convivial institutions for Illich are based on a "radical openness". Illich (1973:57) writes

> I consider conviviality to be individual freedom realized in personal interdependence and, as such, an intrinsic ethical value. I believe that, in any society, as conviviality is reduced below a certain level, no amount of industrial productivity can effectively satisfy the needs it creates among society's members.

Convivial institutions serve 'politically interrelated individuals rather than managers' (Illich 1975: 12) and are characterized by principles of spontaneous use, voluntary participation and universal access that foster forms of association such as peer learning and governance in flat hierarchies. This is the essence of his "learning webs" that he offers as an alternative to compulsory schooling developed some twenty years before the invention of the Internet.

Today with the advent of the Internet and new technologies of openness these principles become the basis of innovative institutional forms that use Web 2.0 and 3.0 technologies to decentralize and democratize power, access to knowledge and relationships. This book is an indication of the virtues of openness (Peters & Roberts, 2011) and its applications in education.

NOTES

[1] See http://www.capetowndeclaration.org/

REFERENCES

Alston, L. J., Eggerston T. & North D. C. (1996). *Empirical Studies of Organizational Change.* Cambridge: Cambridge University Press.

Atkins, D.E., Brown, J.S. & Hammond, A.L. (2007). *A Review of the Open Educational Resources (OER) Movement: Achievements, Challenges, and New Opportunities.* Retrieved from: https://oerknowledgecloud.com/sites/oerknowledgecloud.com/files/ReviewoftheOERMovement.pdf

Benkler, Y. (2006). *The Wealth of Networks: How Social Production Transforms Markets and Freedom,* New Haven, Yale University Press.

Bruns, A. (2008). Blogs, *Wikipedia, Second Life and Beyond: From Production to Produsage,* New York, Peter Lang.

Brunsson, N. & Olsen, J.P. (1993). *The reforming organization.* London and New York: Routledge.

DiMaggio, P.J. & Powell, W.W. (1991). Introduction, in P.J. DiMaggio & W.W. Powell (Eds.), *The new institutionalism in organizational analysis,* pp. 1–38. Chicago: University of Chicago Press.

Foucault, Michel (1977). *Discipline and Punish,* translated by Alan Sheridan, New York: Pantheon.

Foucault, Michel (1980). *Power/Knowledge: Selected Interviews and Other Writings, 1972–1977.* Trans. Colin Gordon et al. New York: Pantheon.

Illich, Ivan (1973). *Deschooling Society,* Harmondsworth: Penguin.

Illich, Ivan (1975). *Tools for Conviviality,* London: Fontana.

Khalil, E. L. (1995). Organizations versus Institutions, *Journal of Institutional and Theoretical Economics, 151,* 445–66.

Laura Brown, Rebecca Griffiths, Matthew Rascoff (2007). The Ithaka Report (2007). *University Publishing In A Digital Age,* Preface: Kevin Guthrie at http://www.ithaka.org/strategicservices/Ithaka%20University%20Publishing%20Report.pdf

March, J.G. & Olsen, J.P. (1984). Retrieved from: http://bss.sfsu.edu/sguo/Renmin/June%2021_institutionalism/New%20Institutionalism_James%20March.pdf

Maxwell, E. (2006, April). *Open Standards, Open Source, and Open Innovation: Harnessing the Benefits of Openness.* Retrieved from: http://www.policyinnovations.org/ideas/policy_library/data/OpenInnovations/_res/id%3Dsa_File1/INNOV0103_p119-176_maxwell.pdf

Miller, Seumas, "Social Institutions", *The Stanford Encyclopedia of Philosophy (Spring 2011 Edition),* Edward N. Zalta (Ed.), http://plato.stanford.edu/archives/spr2011/entries/social-institutions/.

North, Douglass C. (1991). Institutions, *The Journal of Economic Perspectives,* Vol. 5, No. 1 (Winter, 1991), pp. 97–112.

North, Douglass, C. (1990). *Institutions, Institutional Change and Economic Performance,* New York: Cambridge University Press.

OECD (2007). *Giving Knowledge for Free: The Emergence Of Open Educational Resources.* Retrieved from: http://www.oecd.org/dataoecd/35/7/38654317.pdf

OLCOS(2007). *Open Educational Practices and Resources.* Retrieved from: http://www.elearningeuropa. info/files/media/media14907.pdf

Olsen, J. P. & B. G. Peters (1996). Introduction: Learning from Experience?, in J.P. Olsen & B.G. Peters (Eds.), *Lessons from Experience: Experiential Learning from Administrative Reform in Eight Democracies.* Oslo: Scandinavian University Press.

Peters, B. Guy (2000). *Institutional Theory: Problems and Prospects,* Institute for Advanced Studies, Vienna, Political Science Series, 69.

Peters, B.G. (2000). Retrieved from: http://www.google.com/url?sa=t&rct=j&q=&esrc=s&frm=1& source=web&cd=3&ved=0CFgQFjAC&url=http%3A%2F%2Fwww.ihs.ac.at%2Fvienna%2Fpublicat ion.php%3Ftool_e_action%3Ddownload_file%26id%3D336&ei=Yg4BUKzuL46KmQWbvsDrCQ& usg=AFQjCNFw2nuMG46hYgYahfEwIkU8CR5SAg&sig2=WYofDYQL2KcEmZYPK-oEDw

Peters, M.A. & Britize, R.G. (2008). Introduction: Open education and education for openness. In M.A. Peters & R.G. Britize (Eds.) (2008). *Open education and education for openness* (pp. xvii–xxii). Rotterdam, the Netherlands: Sense.

Peters, M.A. & Roberts, Peter (2011). *The Virtues of Openness,* New York, Peter Lang.

Rawls, John (1972). *A Theory of Justice,* Cambridge, MA: Harvard University Press.

Rawls, John (1999). *The Law of Peoples,* Cambridge, MA: Harvard University Press.

Scott, W. R. (1995). *Institutions and Organizations.* Thousand Oaks, CA: Sage.

Turner, Jonathan (1997). *The Institutional Order,* New York: Longman.

Zucker. L. (1987). Institutional Theories of Organizations, *Annual Review of Sociology, 13,* 443–64.

CREATIVE ECONOMY AND OPEN EDUCATION: THE POLITICAL ECONOMY OF OPEN KNOWLEDGE PRODUCTION

Creative economy and open education seem to be two different fields but have a common emphasis on "open knowledge". Moreover, open knowledge can contribute to political economic development. This section includes discussion of open knowledge and how education promotes open knowledge. In addition, peer-to-peer (P2P) relations play an important role in open knowledge production by constructing collective networks in order to create knowledge and innovations. Open knowledge production is an important feature that has emerged from the concepts of creative economies and openness. Open knowledge can also be seen as the main factor that can be expected to promote knowledge economies in the future due to their efficiency and influence on knowledge production.

Creative economies and open education have an interactive relationship with respect to their development and social influences. Creative economies sometimes require the sort of collective knowledge production that open education can provide. On the other hand, open education can be improved with creative economic development, which encourages a culture of openness and improves communication technology. Both may also provide a broader social good by offering opportunities to greater numbers of individuals to acquire knowledge and participate in interactive knowledge creation. More to the point, broad social environments and relationships are critical for the development of open knowledge, and vice versa.

The moral implications of pedagogy also suggest that our responsibility as public intellectuals cannot be separated from the consequences of the knowledge we produce, the social relations we legitimate, and the ideologies and identities we offer to students (Giroux, 2006, p. 69). Open knowledge promotes knowledge production and a type of open culture that encourages openness. This openness can either influence individuals to open their minds and share their thoughts or encourage established interactive networks and open social boundaries.

INTERACTION BETWEEN CREATIVE ECONOMIES AND OPEN EDUCATION

Peters (2010a.) stated that the concept of open innovation helps explain the relationship between creativity and openness. Increasingly complex innovations encourage companies to obtain knowledge from external sources and utilize nonlinear feedback (Teirlinck & Spithoven, 2008; Peters, 2010a.). As complex innovation networks grow, the use of the model of open innovation unlocks the gates for the adoption of knowledge across disciplines and across institutions, so that increasing numbers of knowledge-creating partners are welcomed (Teirlinck & Spithoven, 2008). Creativity can occur in any system that has characteristics of openness (Johnson, 2005). Open education provides opportunities for the production of open collective knowledge. These fulfill the need for open innovation and cross boundaries that exist in creative economies.

The needs of creative economies can also encourage applications of innovative communication technologies. The various aspects of creative economies are often combined with advanced technological applications in order to produce new creations. Creative economies can also encourage the improved usage of technology, including communication technologies. Open education development today refers to improvements in communication technologies. As creative economies develop, they experience an increasing need for open innovation, which leads to open education, which in turn attracts greater public interest and resources, which can improve its effectiveness.

COOPERATION FOR PERSONAL AND SOCIAL GOOD

Combining creative economies and open education can provide personal and social benefits. Encouraging creativity and openness in aspects of either creative economies or open education engenders competition for individuals and society. On one hand, individuals can use open education to obtain and create knowledge, because open education provides access to personal learning, which allows individuals to contribute to creative economies and even profit from them. On the other hand, taking a broader organizational and social perspective, greater numbers of individuals can obtain knowledge and contribute to innovations. Both creative economies and open education encourage collective knowledge, which can spur individual contributions and cooperation in the production of knowledge.

Opening learning opportunities allow individuals to obtain knowledge and can improve human resources on the societal level. Collective knowledge can lead to broader level of cooperative innovations. Richard Luecke (2003) noted that a high percentage of important inventions in organizations are produced by means of collective effort. Being open to new ideas, even in the face of scientific skepticism, is important for organizational creativity (Luecke, 2003). Creative economies and open education provide educational resources for individuals to use. They also provide organizations and societies with an environment that encourages the development of new innovations.

OPEN KNOWLEDGE IN THE PRESENT

Open knowledge on one hand identifies knowledge held openly and is available to all individuals. On the other hand, open knowledge indicates the era of collective cooperation in knowledge production processes. Knowledge is now available to greater numbers of individuals than in the past. As knowledge systems change from esoteric to open, open knowledge represents the future in academic development and democratic societies. As regards research and the academic community, knowledge is increasingly open to critiques and discussion in academic communities. The open attitude, which is characteristic of knowledge systems, encourages the creative development of knowledge. In democratic societies, open knowledge can enlighten the citizenry. Putting democratic ideals into practice requires that individuals understand public issues and become involved in discourse. Given such circumstances, citizens require a certain level of basic knowledge in order to deal with issues and deal with other people when they engage in discourse. Open knowledge can offer individuals the tools and equipment that democratic societies need. The rise of knowledge economies and creative economies has made knowledge increasingly crucial because it has become increasingly synonymous with the ability to compete economically. Peters (2010b.) explained open knowledge as follows:

> Open knowledge production is based upon an incremental, decentralized (and asynchronous), and collaborative development process that transcends the traditional proprietary market model. Commons-based peer production is based on free cooperation, not on the selling of one's labor in exchange for a wage, nor motivated primarily by profit or for the exchange value of the resulting product; it is managed through new modes of peer governance rather than traditional organization hierarchies and it is an innovative application of copyright which creates an information commons and transcends the limitations attached to both private (for-profit) and public (state-based) property forms (Peters, 2010b., pp. 257).

Open knowledge also indicates that knowledge can be shared and created by greater numbers of inclusive individuals. Knowledge serves the public good. Peters (2010b., pp. 254–255) states that knowledge has the following features that serve the global public good:

1. Knowledge is non-rivalrous
2. Knowledge is barely excludable
3. Knowledge is not transparent

Contemporary open knowledge production can be accessed using communication technologies and is supported by the ideas of openness and creative economies. Greater numbers of individuals can participate in the production of open knowledge through technologies such as the Internet. Open knowledge production does not focus exclusively on knowledge-producing outcomes. It also focuses on increasing collective intelligence as a form of input. Increasing collective intelligence requires opening opportunities for more people to become involved, and releasing information and knowledge for more people to absorb. This relates primarily to open education, which can provide resources and opportunities for greater numbers of people and encourage them to interact and create new knowledge products.

THE GROWTH OF CIVILIZATION AND OPEN KNOWLEDGE PRODUCTION

Open knowledge production becomes more inclusive and open to all individuals in part as a byproduct of technological developments. The knowledge economy recognizes knowledge as the basis of innovations that support economic growth, and the production of knowledge has become more crucial. Open knowledge production is influenced by communication technologies and creative economies.

TECHNOLOGICAL DEVELOPMENTS

Developments in communication technologies have influenced open knowledge production by encouraging the creation of open cultures and interactive knowledge. Contemporary technological improvements have influenced industrial and social development. Improvements in information systems have changed the nature of industrial production and have impacted social cultures and network usage. Masuda (1981) stated that technological innovations have changed social economic systems in three ways:

> First, technology does the work once done by man. Second, technology makes possible work that man has been unable to do before. Third, existing social and economic structures have been transformed into new social and economic systems. (Masuda, 1981, p. 59)

Technology influences production processes, including knowledge production and the development of cyber societies. Technological development, particularly in the communication of information—that is—media and the Internet, have changed social and economic structures. O'Reilly[1] (also in Peters, 2010b, p. 253) claimed that the core competencies of Web 2.0 include:

1. Services, not packaged software, with cost-effective scalability
2. Control over unique, hard-to-recreate data sources that become richer as more people use them
3. Trusting users as co-developers
4. Harnessing collective intelligence
5. Leveraging the Long Tail ' through customer self-service
6. Software above the level of a single device
7. Lightweight user interfaces, development models, AND business models

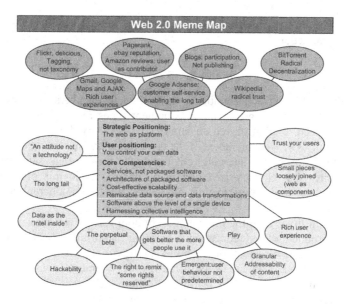

Figure 1. Web 2.0.[2]

This shows a "meme map" of Web 2.0, developed during a brainstorming session at FOO Camp, a conference held by O'Reilly Media.[3] Web 2.0 is an advanced communication technology that influences the culture and practices of open knowledge production. Web 2.0 improves the quality and efficiency of communication, creativity, information sharing, collaboration and the function of communication technology. Openness, innovation, culture, and knowledge-creating communities are phenomena that have been influenced by Web 2.0. Forms of education that make use of technology to promote openness are the result of Web 2.0 (Peters & Britez, 2008), and the open system concept in education has brought forth new possibilities. Wiki-collaboration based on the wisdom of the crowd' (Surowiecki, 2004), mass innovation (Leadbeater, 2009), and inclusive participation and collaboration all encourage the development of social media and networking (Peters, 2009). This technology improvement may enhance the development of open knowledge.

FROM CLOSED SYSTEM TO OPEN SYSTEM

Knowledge production systems include closed and open systems. On one hand, knowledge of various technologies and arts has promoted open knowledge. On the other hand, the kinds of knowledge provided by formal education have often been closed and limited to selected groups throughout recorded history. This section begins with the esoteric system, and focuses on closed educational systems that have existed in the past. The second part focuses on the perspectives of an open system, and involves technology, the development of art, and educational openness. The third part describes changes in the knowledge system and knowledge production.

ESOTERIC SYSTEMS

Education and learning opportunities were limited to members of elites in early human history. Limited transportation in ancient times resulted in homogeneous societies in which religion played an important role. Only those who engaged in religious activities or were members of the upper class had leisure time with which to learn. Such exclusive learning environments were often safeguarded by 'initiation' rites that characterized certain occupations, and this often involved activities, such as protecting secrets and codes that were inherent in esoteric knowledge.

From ancient times until the middle ages, in both eastern and western societies, knowledge production and educational learning opportunities were limited to members of certain classes. For example, in Egypt, learning hieroglyphs was limited to scribes, and in Greek city-states, only liberated (non-slave) citizens enjoyed opportunities for formal learning. In the middle ages, the parish system educated local peasants regarding Christian doctrine and rituals.

Educational changes that offered education to greater numbers of people began to appear. Charles the Great conducted the Carolingian Renaissance,' and Alfred the Great of England encouraged education and the use of the Anglo-Saxon language. However, after their deaths their efforts collapsed. Knowledge acquisition remained limited within esoteric forms. Feudal societies later introduced education in chivalry and developed guilds that involved apprenticeship learning. The foundations of universities were laid during this period. These learning environments were restricted to selected individuals, and some learning environments were more secret and esoteric than others. Some scientific societies remained closed to the public in order to avoid the Church's anti-scientific repression, and the result was that the spread of knowledge remained limited.

In the 16th century, St. Ignatius of Loyola established the Jesuit order and opened hundreds of schools that provided education for Catholics (Cubberley, 1920). Jean Baptiste de la Salle founded the Christian Brothers to provide basic education for members of the peasant classes (Compare, 1900). Johann Heinrich Pestalozzi operated an orphan asylum and focused on educating the youth, which represented a shift of educational interests from adults to children (Compare, 1900).

In many parts of Asia, such as China, educational learning was limited to a certain segment of the population. These were usually people who were studying for government positions. Among members of the general population, the influence of Confucianism led to some schooling for the general population. However, these schools tended to be involved in basic literacy and were not involved in the development and creation of knowledge. The form of education was top-down,' teacher-directed, one-way instruction – not cooperative knowledge creation and openness to knowledge construction, as we would see in the modern era.

Historically speaking, education has generally focused on teaching limited numbers of people limited types of knowledge. This teaching style was typically restricted to one-way instruction and limited forms of knowledge. The knowledge system was exclusive and closed to those outside of that system. This did not change until public school systems were established. Even today, open and interactive teaching-learning environments are found only in some educational systems. During religious revolutions, reform-minded Protestant churches encouraged people to learn to read so that they could read the Bible. The Catholic Church countered by equipping the faithful with literacy so that the general public could enjoy opportunities to learn. These goals and methods of teaching and learning were not directly related to knowledge creation. Knowledge was restricted, controlled by authorities, and remained largely in the hands of churches, governments, and a few members of the elite. Only when democratic societies came into existence did the average person enjoy opportunities to become involved in knowledge creation. Foucault critiqued the relationship of knowledge and power, and knowledge was defined and controlled by authorities. Only after the establishment of democratic societies and post-modernism did knowledge become available to the general public.

OPEN TRADITIONS AND OPEN SYSTEMS

The change from esoteric knowledge to open knowledge and education is related to two major frameworks. One framework is the development of technology; the other is the establishment of democratic societies. The first aspect is the development of technology and its influences. The transformation to open knowledge is due to changes in social institutions and systems and in technological developments that have played an important role in this transformation. Gutenberg's invention of the movable-type printing press amplified the spread of knowledge through the new technology of printed books, which allowed for the sharing of knowledge with large numbers of people. However, although it is true that printing presses reduced the costs of reproducing books, it did not necessarily lead to greater openness. Long (2001) claimed that openness of writing and authorship involved contexts of society, culture, and economics. The educational systems described had long been esoteric in many respects; technology and the arts had long traditions of open culture.

Open knowledge is part of the history of the development of the technical arts. The ancient technē authors wrote in open form and shared with others what they wrote (Long, 2001). In ancient Greece and Rome, the openness praxis writings were shared only by members of certain classes of readers, particularly governors and military leaders (Long, 2001). In the 15th century, open authorship in the mechanical arts expanded (Long, 2001). In the 16th century, materials concerning mining, metallurgy, artillery, and fortifications represented a form of open, and sometimes collective, authorship that included both practitioners and authors

(Long, 2001). Communications about painting, architecture, and the arts also crossed social boundaries, and practitioners and patrons interacted with each other over issues that included learning, technical skills, and art (Long, 2001). The separation of open and secret perspectives were blurred when it came to technological developments. The narrowing of openness in technical manufacturing, and concerns over property and copyrights became part of the culture of the new scientific age. This new scientific age was a sign that intellectual copyrights and property were respected. However, if knowledge systems become too restricted and esoteric, this limits knowledge development and innovation to some degree. Long (2001) argued that the open concepts of the past served as the foundation for experimental science development in the 17th century.

These scientific developments were followed by the Industrial Revolution, which produced two key types of influences on society, which in turn changed the educational systems. First, the economic structures changed when the labor force shifted from farming to industrial production, and this coincided with the development of the welfare system, which provided education for its citizens. Mechanized agriculture could feed more people with fewer laborers. Many people left farms to work in factories in burgeoning cities. New legal restrictions prohibited child labor, and some countries developed mandatory school attendance laws that gave many children opportunities to become educated. For example, in the 18th century Prussia began to require children to attend school, and established a Department for Public Instruction (Monroe, 1970). In England, the Elementary Education Act[4] of 1870 mandated compulsory children's education between the ages of five and twelve. Public education systems were established in modern societies and education became perceived as a human right. Second, the increasingly complex types of work carried out in industrial societies required investments in human capital. Global competition increased government awareness of the value of human recourses. The Knowledge Economy, and the creative economy that came later, emphasized individual intellectual abilities.

The second aspect of open knowledge is the democratic process. In democratic societies, members of the public were able to learn and participate in knowledge production in the context of an open society. More institutions and people became involved in the knowledge-building process, and this became a hallmark of democratic societies. Masuda (1981) stated that the vision of an information society is that every individual can access information and interact through information systems as a manifestation of democracy. Hirsh (1987) claimed that in democratic societies, all citizens require basic knowledge – what Hirsh termed cultural literacy – in order to communicate and become involved in democratic interaction.

Open system theory maintains concepts of openness. Marion (1999) stated that open systems have particular characteristics that include being holistic, interactive, and cybernetic, while adjusting for feedback. Open system perspectives provide the open or cross boundaries, which create interactive relationships among systems and exhibit openness to relationships with other systems. The term—open system describes some important features of open education. An open system can be seen as a nonlinear systematic perspective that involves internal activities, the external environment, and feedback influences. Open system theory claims that external factors, to a greater extent than internal factors, influence internal activities (Marion, 1999). In open education, knowledge construction is open and includes cross-disciplinary participants. Knowledge systems are no longer esoteric and limited, and are now open to collective contributions from people in different disciplines and living systems. Feedback from sources outside of the original system plays an important role in the construction of knowledge.

The continuous development of openness provides the foundation for open knowledge and education in the current era. As technology develops and spreads, democracy encourages open and interactive societies, and open knowledge concepts arise. The next section will examine changes in education and knowledge systems.

THE SHIFT IN EDUCATION AND KNOWLEDGE SYSTEMS IN THE MODERN ERA

Contemporary industrial societies exhibit the influences of commercial media and promote the perspective of open knowledge development. In the 1950s, the U.S. Department of Defense had a research arm then known as the Advanced Research Project Agency (ARPA), which connected different computer networks. What would become known as the Internet' was created in 1969 to connect ten college research laboratories. The commercialization of the Internet changed forms of communication and social interaction. New forms of communication have changed social interactions and decentralized concepts of identity, nationalism, and citizenship (Tukdeo, 2008).

The representative technology is no longer a machine with fixed architecture carrying out a fixed function. It is a system, a network of functionalities—a metabolism of things-executing-things—that can sense its environment and reconfigure its actions to execute appropriately. When a network consists of thousands of separate interacting parts and the environment changes rapidly, it becomes almost impossible to design top-down in any reliable way.

'Therefore, networks are being designed to—learn from experience which simple interactive rules of configuration operate best within different environments' (Arthur, 2009, pp. 206–207).

Technology was not merely a series of mechanical improvements that impelled openness; it also profoundly influenced culture and societies. Heidegger and Foucault thought of technology as a means of revealing truth and influencing human subjectivity (Besley & Peters, 2007). Heidegger thought of technology as a unification of minds, fine arts, and human activities—a process that revealed truth (Heidegger, 1977). Foucault followed Heidegger's perspectives on technology as a way of revealing truth, and extended it to include power relationships and the construction of subjectivity (Besley & Peters, 2007). Derrida's inventionalism referred to open attitudes that added to human interaction and communication, and it was not a mechanical form of openness toward in-coming others (Bista, 2009). Technology became composed more of biological characteristics and fewer mechanistic characteristics for two reasons. First, technologies were simultaneously mechanistic and organic. Second, technologies were acquiring properties that involved self-assembly, self-configuration, self-healing, and cognition, which thus made them resemble living organisms (Arthur, 2009). Open societies and technological developments encouraged individuals to express and construct their own subjectivities.

Changes in technology influenced industrial production processes and knowledge construction. Knowledge construction became open to the public through the Internet and the development of social openness. Democratic societies encouraged the public to attend to public affairs and communicate, which resulted in more people becoming involved in social movements and becoming concerned with public issues. Technological developments facilitated sharing information and communication. Society and technology-based interactions propelled the growth of openness in knowledge production and education.

— 'The theoretical knowledge, the collaborative work style, and the information technologies associated with government-sponsored research and science have indeed become increasingly important elements of society' (Turner, 2006, p. 242).

Creative economies and open education combine with technology to influence social and cultural aspects and can lead to peer-to-peer knowledge production. Gates (2006) used the term Information democracy' to indicate the sharing of free information within the software development process that leads to better knowledge management and changes in the relationship between information and democracy. Information technology has played an important role in social culture. Peters (2007a.) claimed that information has been a central feature of democracies since early social modernized formulation. Benkeler (2003) further stated that political economy has changed as a result of the decentralizing influences that have been brought on by information production. Information changes and supports democratic process of a society.

THE RELATIONSHIP BETWEEN OPEN KNOWLEDGE PRODUCTION AND OPEN EDUCATION

The growing and overlapping concepts of open source, open access, open archiving, and open publishing provide the foundation for openness culture and alternative modes of social production and innovations (Peters, 2010a.). Open knowledge production has become the fundamental concept of open education. Peer-to-peer (P2P) is an important characteristic of relationships for integrating open knowledge production and open education.

OPEN KNOWLEDGE PRODUCTION IS A BASIC IDEA IN OPEN EDUCATION

Open knowledge production is a fundamental concept in open education, one that results from the openness culture and collective knowledge production. The openness culture that derives from open knowledge production is a core concept in open education.

The concept of open knowledge production provides a basic theoretical framework and practical applications for open education. The open and collaborative elements of open knowledge production also serve the fundamental needs of open education. Open and collaborative cultures of knowledge production are rooted in peer review culture and have been transformed into a perspective of open knowledge. First, the peer review culture of the academic world respects self-evaluation and quality improvements in the academic community that are related to openness, changing ideals and procedures, and critical perspectives. Open knowledge production is recognized as being related to open science concepts. Peters (2007b.) stated that global and open science is changing the world to the extent that the era of scientific superpowers may be coming to an end (Hollingsworth, et al, 2008). David (2003) wrote about the origins of open systems in intellectual property32. The following quote comes from his article summary about—The Economic Logic of Open Science'⁵:

> Open science' institutions provide an alternative to the intellectual property approach to dealing with difficult problems in the allocation of resources for the production and distribution of information. As a mode of generating reliable knowledge,—open science depends upon a specific nonmarket reward system to solve a number of resource allocation problems that have their origins in the particular characteristics of information as an economic good....the collegiate reputational reward system...[has been]... conventionally associated with open science practice in the academy and public research institutes...open science is properly regarded as uniquely well suited to the goal of maximizing the rate of growth of the stock of reliable knowledge.

Open knowledge production can be examined from the perspectives of open science to include different aspects of knowledge disciplines. Open knowledge production encourages open and collective intellectual knowledge creation. This process provides open education with a model for knowledge production and learning. This encourages individual intellectual contributions and increases knowledge capital.

PEER TO PEER (P2P) KNOWLEDGE PRODUCTION IN OPEN EDUCATION

Open knowledge production based on collective knowledge production is a practical form of open education. Peer to Peer (P2P) is a approach in which open knowledge production can be used in open education. Improvements in openness and communication make—peer-to-peer (P2P) interactions more effective. Within this P2P network, knowledge becomes more productive (with the use of cooperative production) and can transform open knowledge production into open education practices.

Open knowledge imparts an open attitude to the construction of knowledge. Gates (2006) uses the term—information democracy" to indicate that software development increases the free sharing of information, leads to better knowledge management and changes the relationship between information and democracy. Information technology plays several important roles in social culture. Information is an important influence on democratic society development for individual interaction and the means of political economy (Peters, 2007a; Benkler, 2003). Benkler (2006) stated that changes in information technologies change how individuals interact with information, knowledge and culture, and how such changes affect human freedom. Benkler and Nissenbaum (2006) argued that based on communication technology peer production offers opportunities for more people to produce informational goods as well as opportunities to practice socially responsible behavior. The socio-technical system may involve moral and political values (Benkler and Nissenbaum, 2006). These changes promote the production of open knowledge, as well as practical applications, such as Peer-to-Peer (P2P) productions.

P2P productions are a practical aspect of open knowledge production and an application that can be used in open education. As regards P2P, Bauwens (2010) stated:

> Global communication has shown itself capable of being hyper-productive in creation of complex knowledge products, free and open source software, and increasingly, open design associated with distributed manufacturing. In other words, a hybrid form of production has emerged that combines the existence of global self-managed open design communities, for-benefit associations in the form of foundations that manage the infrastructure of cooperation, and an ecology of associated businesses that benefit from and contribute to this commons-based peer production. (p. 311)

Open knowledge production is based on openness and collective intelligence. In addition, collective knowledge requires participation. Peer networking encourages participation and positive production output. New relationships among societies, enterprises, and individuals become established within this peer network. Bauwens used the term "New Social Contract" to explain the changes in these new relationships. Bauwens' "New Social Contract" includes:

1. Expanding entrepreneurship to civil society and the base of the [social] pyramid
2. New institutions that do well by doing good (outcome-based enterprises)
3. Social financing mechanisms based on peer-to-peer aggregation
4. Mechanisms that sustain social innovation (co-design, co-creation) and peer production by civil society
5. Participatory businesses and other organizations focus on localized, precision-based physical production in small series that are nevertheless linked to global open-design communities. (Bauwens, 2010, pp. 311–312)

Within the context of this new social contract, the basis of socioeconomic development is P2P relationships. The P2P social process helps to create the following factors:

1. **Peer production**: Occurs when a group of peers decides to engage in production from common resource.

2. **Peer governance**: Peers choose to govern themselves while engaging in such pursuits.
3. **Peer property**: The institutional and legal framework they choose guards against the private appropriation of common work. This usually takes the form of non-exclusionary forms of universal common property, as defined through the General Public License, some forms of the Creative Commons Licenses, or similar derivatives (Bauwens, 2010, p. 313).

SERVE THE PUBLIC GOOD AND ACT AS A FORM OF SOCIAL BUSINESS

Collective knowledge production that arises from creative economies and open education can serve the public good. The idea of collective knowledge production can be applied to social business concepts. There are two methods for analyzing this relationship. The first methods of analyzing this idea uses the direct perspective, in which open knowledge is given to everyone so that even the poor and marginalized can learn how to change their economic situation. The second method of analyzing this idea involves using knowledge as capital, because collective knowledge impels institutions with knowledge capital to invest in those that have less knowledge capital.

The concepts of social business require an explanation. Yunus (2008; 2010) stated that social businesses have certain requirements:

1. Social objectives: They should have positive social objectives.
2. Profit distribution: Investors cannot take profits out of enterprises as dividends.
3. Businesses can be classified as social businesses if they are owned by those in poverty, so that making profits promotes the social objectives of the businesses.

Ideally, social businesses should be owned by disadvantaged or poor people so that the disadvantaged or poor are aided in escaping poverty. As regards the first perspective (of offering knowledge to individuals), creative economies and open education can provide knowledge capital to every individual. Knowledge is the key element for competing in the global society.

When viewing knowledge as a form of capital, investing in knowledge can be seen as a type of social business. Peters (2007b) stated that knowledge capitalism concerns understanding knowledge and its value within the context of social relationships. Institutions with surplus knowledge capital are able to act as entrepreneurs that invest in those who lack knowledge capital. Knowledge production can thus serve as a public good (Samuelson, 1954; Marginson, 2007; Marginson, 2009). Marginson (2007) argued that the global public good and private goods in higher education are not zero-sum games, but rather, are often interdependent. However, there remains limitation regarding knowledge access and creation. Institutions with greater amounts of knowledge capital can invest in the disadvantaged or the knowledge-poor. Knowledge-poor individuals may improve their status by accepting knowledge investments. This can help bring about improvement in entire socioeconomic levels of knowledge.

CONCLUSION

Open knowledge production is a form that combines openness culture and collaborative intelligence. Knowledge-producing systems have changed throughout history and through the course of various philosophical perspectives. Openness perspectives and improvements in communication technologies have encouraged open knowledge production. Open knowledge production encourages collective and collaborative knowledge interactions and production among individuals.

Open education is a form of open knowledge production application. Open education has developed in conjunction with open concepts and improvements in communication technology. The relationship between open knowledge production and open education is such that open knowledge provides the underlying concepts that support open education. P2P is a practical aspect of open knowledge production that can imply the existence of open education.

NOTES

[1] O'Reilly explained Web 2.0, Retrieved Nov., 18, 2010, from: http://oreilly.com/pub/a/web2/archive/what-is-web-20.html?page=1

[2] O'Reilly explained Web 2.0, Retrieved Nov., 18, 2010, from: http://oreilly.com/pub/a/web2/archive/what-is-web-20.html?page=5

[3] Web 2.0, Retrieved Nov., 18, 2010, from: http://oreilly.com/web2/archive/what-is-web-20.html

[4] UK, Elementary Education Act. Retrieved May, 3, 2011, from: http://www.thepotteries.org/dates/education.htm

[5] The conference Science in the 21st Century. Retrieved Jan., 10, 2011, from: http://www.science21stcentury.org /abstracts.html

REFERENCES

Arthur, W.B. (2009). *The nature of technology*. New York, NY: Free Press.

Bauwens, M. (2010). Toward a P2P Economy, in D. Araya & M.A. Peters (Eds.) (2010). *Education in the creative economy: Knowledge and learning in the age of innovation* (pp. 305–330). New York: NY: Peter Lang.

Benkler, Y. & Nissenbaum, H. (2006). Commons-based Peer Production and Virtue, *The journal of political philosophy, 14*(4), pp. 394–419.

Benkler, Y. (2003). *Freedom in the commons: Toward a political economy of information.* Retrieved from http://www.law.duke.edu/shell/cite.pl?52+Duke+L.+J.+1245

Benkler, Y. (2006). *The wealth of networks: How social production transforms markets and freedom.* New Haven, CT: Yale University Press.

Besita, G. (2009). Education between accountability and responsibility, in M. Simons, M. Olssen, M.A. Peters (Eds.), *Re-reading education policies: A hand book studying the policy agenda of the 21st century*, pp. 650–666. Rotterdam, The Netherlands: Sense.

Besley, A.C. & Peters, M.A. (2007). *Subjectivity and truth: Foucault, education, and the culture of self.* New York: Peter Lang.

Compayre, G. (1900). *The history of pedagogy*. London, UK: Swan Sonnenschein.

Cubberley, E. (1920). *The history of education: Educational practice and progress considered as a phase of the development and spread of Western civilization*. Boston, MA: Houghton Mifflin.

David, P. A. (2003). The Economic Logic of 'Open Science' and the Balance between Private Property Rights and the Public Domain in Scientific Data and Information: A Primer, Retrieved from: http://siepr.stanford.edu/publicationsprofile/445.

Gates, B. (2006). The Road Ahead. *Newsweek*, Jan. 25, 2006. Retrieved from: http://www.msnbc.msn.com/id/11020787/

Giroux, H.A. (2006). Public pedagogy and the politics of Neoliberalism: Making the political more pedagogical, in A. Dirlik (Ed.) (2006). *Pedagogies of the global: Knowledge in human interests*, pp. 59–76. Boulder, CO: Paradigm.

Heidegger, M. (1977). *The Question Concerning Technology and Other Essays*, W. Lovitt (trans.), New York, NY: Garland.

Hirsch, E.D. (1987). *Cultural literacy, what every American needs to know*. Boston, MA. Houghton Mifflin Company.

Hollingsworth, J., Rogers, M., Karl H. & Hollingsworth, E.J. (2008). End of science superpowers? *Nature, 454*, 412–413.

Johnson, C. (2005). *Varieties of openness in evolutionary creativity*. Retrieved from http://kar.kent.ac.uk/14358/1/VarietiesColin.pdf.

Leadbeater, C. (2008). *We-Think: The Power of Mass Creativity*. London, UK: Profile Books.

Long, P.O. (2001). *Openness, secrecy, authorship: Technical arts and the culture of knowledge from antiquity to the renaissance*. Baltimore, MA: The John Hopkins University Press.

Luecke, R. (2003). *Managing creativity and innovation: Practical strategies to encourage creativity*. Boston, MA: Harvard Business School.

Marginson, S. (2007). The new higher education landscape: Public and private goods, in global/national/local settings, in S. Marginson (Ed.), *Prospects of higher educations* (pp. 29–77). Rotterdam, the Netherlands: Sense.

Marginson, S. (2009). University ranking and the knowledge economy. In M.A. Peters, S. Marginson, & P. Murphy. *Creativity and the global knowledge economy* (pp. 185–217). New York, NY: Peter Lang.

Marion, R. (1999). *The edge of organization: chaos and complexity theories of formal social system*. London, UK: Sage.

Masuda, Y. (1981). *The information society as post-industrial society*. Bethesda, MD: World Future Society.

Monroe, P.A. (1970). *Text-Book in the History of Education*, New York: Ams Press.

Peters, M.A. & Britize, R.G. (2008). Introduction: Open education and education for openness. In M.A. Peters & R.G.Britize (Eds.) (2008). *Open education and education for openness* (pp. xvii–xxii). Rotterdam, the Netherlands: Sense.

Peters, M.A. (2007a). The political economy of informational democracy, in C. Kaptizke and M.A. Peters (Eds.) (2007). *Global knowledge cultures* (pp. 209–221), Rotterdam, The Netherland: Sense.

Peters, M.A. (2007b). *Knowledge economy, development and the future of higher education*. Rotterdam, The Netherlands: Sense.

Peters, M.A. (2009). *The Changing Architecture of Global Science*, Retrieved from https://www.ideals.illinois.edu/handle/2142/10682

Peters, M.A. (2010a). Creativity, openness, and user-generated culture, in D. Araya & M.A. Peters (Eds.) (2010). *Education in the creative economy: Knowledge and learning in the age of innovation*, pp. 203–224. New York, NY: Peter Lang.

Peters, M. A. (2010b.). The Rise of global science and emerging political economy of international research collaborations, in S. Marinson, P. Murphy, & M. A. Peters (Eds.) (2010). *Global creation: Space, mobility and synchrony in the age of the knowledge economy*, pp. 229–248, New York, NY: Peter Lang.

Samuelson, P. (1954). The pure theory of public expenditure. *Review of economics and statistics, 36*(4), 387–389.

Surowiecki, J. (2004). *The wisdom of crowds: Why the many are smarter than the few and how collective wisdom shapes business, economies, societies and nations*. New York, NY: Doubleday.

Teirlinck, P. & Spithoven, A. (2008). The spatial organization of innovation: Open innovation, external knowledge relations and urban structure. *Regional Studies, 42*(5), pp. 689–704.

Tukdeo, S. (2008). The power of P2P: Information networks, social organizing and education futures. In M. A. Peters & R. G. Britez. (Eds.) (2008). *Open education and education for openness*, pp. 43–55. Rotterdam, the Netherlands: Sense.

Turner, F. (2006). *From counterculture to cyberculture: Steward, the whole earth network, and the rise of digital utopianism*. Chicago, IL: The University of Chicago Press.

Yunus, M. (2008). *Creating a world without poverty: Social business and the future of capitalism*. New York, NY: Public Affairs.

Yunus, M. (2010). *Building Social Business: The new kind of capitalism that serves humanity's most pressing needs*. New York, NY: Public Affairs.

CREATIVITY, OPENNESS AND THE GLOBAL KNOWLEDGE ECONOMY: THE ADVENT OF USER-GENERATED CULTURES

INTRODUCTION

This chapter investigates the relation between creativity and the global knowledge economy focusing on the characteristics of knowledge as a global public good and digital information goods in so far as they approach 'pure thought'. The chapter then explores the relations between openness and creativity through a review of the literature and by reference to 'social creativity' as evidenced in user-generated cultures.

CREATIVITY AND THE GLOBAL KNOWLEDGE ECONOMY[1]

The global knowledge economy, comprised of increasingly integrated cross-border distributed knowledge and learning systems, represents a new stage of development that is characterized by a fundamental sociality – knowledge and the value of knowledge are rooted in social relations. More than any time in the past, the global economy and society are undergoing a massive transformation from an industrial age that was dominated by the logic of standardized mass production and epitomized by the assembly-line in the auto-industry to a knowledge economy that is characterized by decentralized networked communications. These communication systems reflect "intellectual capital" in a range of information-service industries that are propelled by brainpower and the constant demand for innovation. These innovations do not mean the demise of the industrial economy but rather the development of a new relation between manufacturing and information services that permit the sharing of knowledge through open source models and the continuous redesign of flexible production regimes. It also means the rapid development of "mind-intensive" industries, especially in the software, media, healthcare, education, and other mind-intensive industries. Increasingly, the move to the knowledge economy redefines the value creation process, alters the organization and pattern of work, and creates new forms of borderless cooperation and intercultural exchange. This dynamic has led many national government and international organizations to plan for a restructuring of the economy that increasingly focuses on knowledge, education, and creativity. The New Club of Rome, for instance, calls this new era the paradigm of an "economy of the intangibles" and predicts "Third Phase Industries," "sustainable development" and the development of "intellectual capital":

- This trend means that the intellectual, social, and cultural issues require much higher attention. They are the determinants of Third Phase Industries based on creativity, software, media, finance, services, and, more generally, combined intelligence. These qualities are more representative of today's developed economies, and they produce more value than traditional manufacturing per se. They are of decisive importance to the development of all sectors, including traditional ones. Only through careful and sustainable utilization of the new, nonmaterial resources will we be in a position to better organize material and energy resources that are increasingly in short supply.
- More specifically the "Ever More" of the current economic model of the Western industrial society has outlived its legitimacy. What matters are not mere survival strategies or linear expansion, but rather sustainable preservation so that we can retain our prosperity. In order to master the future, we need more intelligent modes of cultivation and exploitation and a new balance between material and nonmaterial resources.
- Intellectual capital (comprising assets such as human abilities, structural, relational, and innovation capital, as well as social capital) founded on clear, practiced values such as integrity, transparency, cooperation ability, and social responsibility, constitute the basic substance from which our future society will nurture itself.[2]

The postindustrial society, a term invented by Arthur Penty, a British Guild Socialist and follower of William Morris, at the turn from the nineteenth to the twentieth century, was based on craft workshop and decentralized units of government. The postindustrial society is marked by the change from a goods-producing to a service economy and the widespread diffusion of "intellectual technologies." For Daniel Bell (1973) the concept of post-industrialism dealt primarily with changes *in the social structure* including the shift from a goods-producing economy to a service economy, the centrality of theoretical knowledge for innovation, the change in the character of work, and the shift from a game against nature to a game among persons. His early account given in the 1970s – before the invention of the Internet and the spread of communications networks – did not foresee the phenomenon of virtualization or the emergence of personalization as a 24/7 totally person-centered, unique learning environment (Peters, 2009a).

Although there are different readings and accounts of the knowledge economy, it was only when the OECD (1996) used the label in the mid-1990s and it was adopted as a major policy description/prescription and strategy by the United Kingdom in 1999 that the term passed into the policy literature and became acceptable and increasingly widely used. The "creative economy" is an adjunct policy term based on many of the same economic arguments – and especially the centrality of theoretical knowledge and the significance of innovation. Most definitions highlight the growing relative significance of knowledge compared with traditional factors of production – natural resources, physical capital and low-skill labor – in wealth creation and the importance of knowledge creation as a source of competitive advantage to all sectors of the economy, with a special emphasis on R&D, higher education and knowledge-intensive industries such as the media and entertainment. At least two sets of principles distinguish knowledge goods, in terms of their behavior, from other goods, commodities, or services; the first set concerns Knowledge as a Global Public Good—close to Peters 2010 in Global Creation or 2009 Creativity and the Global knowledge economy; the second concerns the digitalization of knowledge goods.

These features have led a number of economists to hypothesize the knowledge economy and to picture it as different from the traditional industrial economy, leading to a structural transformation. In *The Economics of Knowledge* (2004) Dominique Foray argues:

> Some, who had thought that the concepts of a new economy and a knowledge-based economy related to more or less the same phenomenon, logically concluded that the bursting of the speculative high-tech bubble sealed the fate of a short-lived knowledge-based economy. My conception is different. I think that the term 'knowledge-based economy' is still valid insofar as it characterizes *a possible scenario of structural transformations of our economies.* This is, moreover, the conception of major international organizations such as the World Bank and the Organisation for Economic Cooperation and Development (OECD). (p. ix, emphasis added).

In this scenario "the rapid creation of new knowledge and the improvement of access to the knowledge bases thus constituted, in every possible way (education, training, transfer of technological knowledge, diffusion of innovations), are factors increasing economic efficiency, innovation, the quality of goods and services, and equity between individuals, social categories, and generations." He goes on to argue that there is a collision between two phenomena – "a long-standing trend, reflected in the expansion of 'knowledge-related' investments" and "a unique technological revolution."

KNOWLEDGE AS A GLOBAL PUBLIC GOOD

The first set of principles concerning knowledge as an economic good indicate that knowledge defies traditional understandings of property and principles of exchange and closely conforms to the criteria for a public good:

1. knowledge is *non-rivalrous*: the stock of knowledge is not depleted by use, and in this sense knowledge is not consumable; sharing with others, use, reuse, and modification may indeed add rather than deplete value;
2. knowledge is barely *excludable*: it is difficult to exclude users and to force them to become buyers; it is difficult, if not impossible, to restrict distribution of goods that can be reproduced with no or little cost;
3. knowledge is not *transparent*: knowledge requires some experience of it before one discovers whether it is worthwhile, relevant, or suited to a particular purpose.

Thus, knowledge at the *ideation* or *immaterial* stage considered as pure ideas operates expansively to defy the law of scarcity. It does not conform to the traditional criteria for an economic good, and the economics of knowledge is, therefore, not based on an understanding of those features that characterize property or exchange and cannot be based on economics as the science of the allocation of scarce public goods. Of course, as soon as knowledge becomes codified or written down or physically embedded in a system or process, it can be made subject to copyright or patent and then may be treated and behave like other commodities (Stiglitz, 1999a).

DIGITAL INFORMATION GOODS APPROXIMATING PURE THOUGHT

The second set of principles apply to digital information goods insofar as they approximate pure thought or the ideational stage of knowledge, insofar as data and information through experimentation and hypothesis testing (the traditional methods of sciences) can be turned into justified true belief. In other words, digital information goods also undermine traditional economic assumptions of rivalry, excludability, and transparency, as the knowledge economy is about creating intellectual capital rather than accumulating physical capital. Digital information goods differ from traditional goods in a number of ways:

1. Information goods, especially in digital forms, can be copied cheaply, so there is little or no cost in adding new users. Although production costs for information have been high, developments in desktop and just-in-time publishing, together with new forms of copying, archiving and content creation, have substantially lowered fixed costs.
2. Information and knowledge goods typically have an experiential and participatory element that increasingly requires the active co-production of the reader/writer, listener and viewer.
3. Digital information goods can be transported, broadcast, or shared at low cost, which may approach free transmission across bulk communication networks.
4. Since digital information can be copied exactly and easily shared, it is never consumed (see Varian, 1998; Morris-Suzuki, 1997; Davis & Stack, 1997; Kelly, 1998).

The implication of this brief analysis is that the laws of supply and demand that depend on the scarcity of products do not apply to digital information goods.

CREATING THE CREATIVE ECONOMY

Today there is a strong renewal of interest by politicians and policy-makers worldwide in the related notions of creativity and innovation, especially in relation to terms like "the creative economy," "knowledge economy," "enterprise society," "entrepreneurship," and "national systems of innovation" (Baumol, 2002; Cowen, 2002; Lash & Urry, 1994). In its most obvious form the notion of the creative economy emerges from a set of claims that suggests that the Industrial Economy is giving way to the Creative Economy based on the growing power of ideas and virtual value – the turn from steel and hamburgers to software and intellectual property (Florida, 2002; Howkins, 2001; Landry, 2000).

In this context increasingly policy latches onto the issues of copyright as an aspect of IP, piracy, distribution systems, network literacy, public service content, the creative industries, new interoperability standards, the WIPO and the development agenda, WTO and trade, and means to bring creativity and commerce together (Cowen, 2002; Shapiro & Varian, 1998; Davenport & Beck, 2001; Hughes, 1988; Netanel, 1996, 1998; Gordon, 1993; Lemley, 2005; Wagner, 2003). At the same time, this focus on creativity has exercised strong appeal to policy-makers who wish to link education more firmly to new forms of capitalism emphasizing how creativity must be taught, how educational theory and research can be used to improve student learning in mathematics, reading and science, and how different models of intelligence and creativity can inform educational practice (Blythe, 2000).

Under the spell of the creative economy discourse, there has been a flourishing of new accelerated learning methodologies together with a focus on giftedness the design of learning programs for exceptional children.[3] One strand of the emerging literature highlights the role of the creative and expressive arts, of performance, of aesthetics in general, and the significant role of design as an underlying infrastructure for the creative economy (Caves, 2000; Frey, 2000; Frey & Pommerehne, 1989; Ginsburgh & Menger, 1996; Heilbron & Gray, 2001; Hesmondhalgh, 2002). There is now widespread agreement among economists, sociologists, and policy analysts that creativity, design, and innovation are at the heart of the global knowledge economy: together creativity, design, and innovation define knowledge capitalism and its ability to continuously reinvent itself.[4] Together and in conjunction with new communications technologies, they give expression to the essence of digital capitalism – the "economy of ideas" – and to new architectures of mass collaboration that distinguish it as a new generic form of economy different in nature from industrial capitalism.

The fact is that knowledge in its immaterial digitized informational form as sequences and value chains of 1s and 0s – ideas, concepts, functions, and abstractions –approaches the status of pure thought. Unlike other commodities, it operates expansively to defy the law of scarcity that is fundamental to classical and neoclassical economics and to the traditional understanding of markets. As mentioned above a generation of economists has expressed this truth by emphasizing that knowledge is (almost) a global public good: it is non-rivalrous and barely excludable (Stiglitz, 1999b; Verschraegen & Schiltz, 2007). It is non-rivalrous in the sense that there is little or only marginal cost to adding new users. In other words, knowledge and information, especially in digital form, cannot be consumed. The use of knowledge or information as digital goods can be distributed and shared at no extra cost, and the distribution and sharing is likely to add to its value rather than to deplete it or use it up. This is the essence of the economics of file-sharing education; it is also the essence of new forms of distributed creativity, intelligence and innovation in an age of mass participation and collaboration (Brown & Duguid, 2000; Tapscott & Williams, 2006; Surowiecki, 2004).

OPENNESS AND CREATIVITY

There is a long established literature on openness and creativity in the field of personality psychology emphasizing the uniqueness of the individual. Prabhu et al. (2008, p. 53), for instance, report that four decades of work have generated more than 9,000 published studies. They also report that in the five-factor model of personality – based on openness to experience, conscientiousness, extraversion, agreeableness, and neuroticism – "openness to experience has the most empirical support as being closely related to creativity." In this context, openness is correlated with the appreciation for art, emotionality, sense of adventure, new ideas, imagination, curiosity, and variety of experience. On this psychological reading open people prefer novelty and change, and tend to be more aware of their feelings with a corresponding willingness to tolerate diversity and entertain new ideas. Those people with "closed" personality, by contrast, tend to exhibit more traditional and conventional interests and prefer familiarity over novelty and change. The five-factor personality psychology is purely descriptive rather than theory driven, and current research is testing the cross-cultural and social validity of the program. While it is still in progress, this research at least raises the strong possibility of the close correlation of openness with creativity at the level of individual personalities emphasizing the relation to concepts of measured intelligence, achievement, and political attitudes (Simonton, 2000; Aitken, 2004; Dollinger, 2007).

Individualist approaches to the relation of openness to creativity can only take us so far. The National Academy of Sciences' (2003) report *Beyond Productivity: Information Technology, Innovation and Creativity*, began by recognizing the crucial role that creativity plays in culture and the way in which at the beginning of the twenty-first century, "information technology (IT) is forming a powerful alliance with creative practices in the arts and design to establish the exciting new domain of information technology and creative practices." Others such as Richard Florida (2004) have emphasized that the United States needs to invest more in the development of its creative sector as a basis to sustain its competitiveness from the rate of technological innovation and economic growth. Florida (2002, p. 21) argues "human creativity as the defining feature of economic life... . [New] technologies, new industries, new wealth and all other good economic things flow from it," and he goes on to write "[Human] creativity is multifaceted and multidimensional. It is not limited to technological innovation or new business models. It is not something that can be kept in a box and trotted out when one arrives at the office. Creativity involves distinct kinds of thinking and habits that must be cultivated both in the individual and in the surrounding society" (p. 22). Rutten and Gelissen (2008) test Florida's creativity and diversity hypothesis for European regions, and their results indicate that regional differences in diversity are directly related to differences in wealth between regions.

The relation between openness and creativity is brought out even more forcefully through the concept and practice of open innovation. Peter Teirlinck and Andre Spithoven (2008) indicate that the increasing complexity of innovation has encouraged companies to use external knowledge sources to complement in-house activities, attempting to substitute a nonlinear feedback model for the old linear model, capturing the benefits of the learning process within and between firms and other organizations. As innovation networks grew even more complex, firms adopted the "new imperative" for creating and profiting from technology in the model of open innovation where innovation becomes increasingly distributed among various partners (Von Hippel, 1988). They write:

> The notion of open innovation is the result of the increasing complexity of innovation and how innovation management should cope with this complexity. It reflects an ever changing research environment (Chesbrough, 2001): the increasing mobility of knowledge workers; the applicability of research results of universities to enterprises; more widely distributed knowledge; erosion of oligopoly market positions; more deregulation and an increase in venture capital. This resulted in an open stage gate process with the following features: (1) the centralized inhouse R&D laboratory is no longer the main source of ideas or knowledge and is being complemented by other enterprises, new technology based start-ups, universities, and public research centres; (2) commercialization also occurs outside the traditional markets of the enterprise through licensing, spin-offs, and research joint ventures; (3) the role of the first mover advantage becomes more important than the development of a defensively orientated system of knowledge and technology protection. (p. 689)

This model of open innovation is made possible through "creativity support tools" that help to accelerate discovery and innovation. Ben Shneiderman (2007) notes that new "generations of programming, simulation, information visualization, and other tools are empowering engineers and scientists just as animation and music composition tools have invigorated filmmakers and musicians." He goes on to write:

> These and many other creativity support tools enable discovery and innovation on a broader scale than ever before; eager novices are performing like seasoned masters and the grandmasters are producing startling results. The accelerating pace of academic research, engineering innovation, and consumer product design is amply documented in journal publications, patents, and customer purchases Creativity support tools extend users' capability to make discoveries or inventions from early stages of gathering information, hypothesis generation, and initial production, through the later stages of refinement, validation, and dissemination.

The sustainability of "social creativity" depends upon a greater recognition of the importance of social and material surroundings. As Fischer and Giaccardi (2007) argue "Individual and social creativity can and must complement each other." They suggest:

> Environments supporting mass collaboration and social production such as annotated collections (GenBank), media sharing (Flickr, YouTube), wikis (Wikipedia), folksonomies (del.icio.us), and virtual worlds (Second Life) are other examples of social creativity. The diverse and collective stock of scientific content and artistic or stylistic ideas that individuals and communities share, reinterpret, and use as a basis for new ideas and visions constitutes the vital source of invention and creativity.

They argue that creativity needs the "synergy of many" which can be facilitated by meta-design – "a sociotechnical approach that characterizes objectives, techniques, and processes that allow users to act as designers and be creative in personally meaningful activities," and they note a tension between creativity and organization. Organizational environments must be kept open to users' modifications and adaptations by technical and social means that empower participation to serve the double purpose: "to provide a potential source for new insights, new knowledge, and new understandings; and to provide a higher degree of synergy and self-organization."

The relationship between creativity and open systems especially in computing is growing in significance. Colin G. Johnson (2005) draws a strong set of connection between openness, creativity, and search processes. He begins by noting that "One characteristic of systems in which creativity can occur is that they are open. That is, the space being explored appears to be (theoretically or pragmatically) unbounded, and there is no easy way in which the structure of the space can be simply summarized." He suggests that evolutionary search processes (moving from one-to-point, using the information from previously visited sites) are seen as creative for one of three reasons:

> Firstly because the criteria for evaluation are not easy to capture in a rulebound fashion. An example of this is searching a space of melodies for 'interesting' or 'tuneful' melodies. Secondly because the search space is seen as having some complexity which belies 'easy' search. Examples of this [sic] ideas include the use of search to explore the space of designs for mechanical devices or electrical circuits. Even though an exhaustive search would turn up the same result as a 'creative' search, both the size of the search space and the complex structure thereof (e.g. it is not possible for a 'naïve' thinker to conceive of how to specify and order the 'all possible' designs). Thirdly, because the search space is seen as being extensible. Consider the idea of searching a space of melodies as discussed above. In order to search this space, we will need to give a description of what a 'melody' is – e.g. a sequence of notes in a particular key. However this definition has limitations: what about a melody that changes key half way through? So we expand the search space to include such melodies, then... . The search space can always be extended. It is these latter two characteristics which seem particularly to

capture the idea of 'openness' in creativity. (http://kar.kent.ac.uk/14358/1/VarietiesColin.pdf)

Open source in computing developed around Linux as an operating system where in such open systems intellectual property is seen as "open" and is made freely available, allowing people to use ideas and code without locking them up as private intellectual property. It is based on three essential features (Tippet, 2007, updated from Weber, 2004):

- source code is distributed with the software, or made available at no more cost than distribution (this means that users can see and change the actual mechanisms that makes the software work);
- anyone may distribute the software for free (there is not obligation for other users of the software to pay royalties or licensing fees to the originator);
- anyone may modify the software, or develop new software from the original product, and the modified software is then distributed under the same terms as the original software (e.g., it remains open).

As Weber comments these concepts represent a fundamentally different concept of property, typically seen as:

a regime built around a set of assumptions and goals that are different from those of mainstream intellectual property rights thinking. The principal goal of the open source intellectual property regime is to maximize the ongoing use, growth, development, and distribution of free software. To achieve that goal, this regime shifts the fundamental optic of intellectual property rights away from the protecting the prerogatives of an author towards protecting the prerogatives of generations of users. (Weber, 2004, p. 84)

The idea of open source still retains concepts of copyright and the rights of the author or creator over their original work. As Tippet (2007) remarks: "It does thus not negate the concept of property within intellectual products, but rather shifts the view of the rights conferred by the property, so that the 'concept of property [is] configured around the right and responsibility to distribute, not to exclude' (Weber 2004: 86)." Tippet also usefully documents the emerging field that applies open source to areas of scholarship and creative endeavor outside software:

For example, open source has been explored as a valuable approach in scientific endeavour and making scientific information available (Jones 2001; Mulgan 2005; Schweik, C., Evans and Grove 2005). Keats (2003) has explored open source in terms of developing teaching and learning resources for African universities'. In a series of articles looking at the 'Adaptive State', the potential value of open source ideas for public policy delivery are explored (Bentley and Wilsdon 2003; Leadbeater 2003; Mulgan, Salem and Steinberg 2005). The ideas have been developed in product design, linked to ideas of open innovation, as companies engage with user communities (Goldman and Gabriel 2005), one example being user-led innovation in sports gear (Fuller, Jawecki and Muhlbacher 2007).

Digital technologies have become engines of cultural innovation and user-centered content production has become a sign of the general transformation of organizational forms. However, the transformation of digital culture also transforms "what it means to be a creator within a vast and growing reservoir of media, data, computational power, and communicative possibilities." We are only now beginning to devise understandings of the power of databases, network representations, filtering techniques, digital rights management, and the other new architectures of agency and control and "how these new capacities transform our shared cultures, our understanding of them, and our capacities to act within them" (Karaganis, 2008).

As Jean Burgess (2007) comments in *Vernacular Creativity and the New Media* "The manufacturers of content-creating tools, who relentlessly push us to unleash that creativity, using – of course – their ever cheaper, ever more powerful gadgets and gizmos. Instead of asking consumers to watch, to listen, to play, to passively consume, the race is on to get them to create, to produce, and to participate" (p. 7). She goes on to register the development of a new vocabulary that speaks of a participatory culture based on creation and user-generated content.

> In game environments particularly, terms like 'co-creators' (Banks, 2002) and 'productive players' (Humphreys, 2005) are increasingly gaining purchase as replacements for 'consumers', 'players', or even 'participants'. These reconfigurations force us to consider the 'texts' of new media to be emergent – always in the process of being 'made'; further, 'co-creation' is built around network sociality and the dynamics of community, prompting a reconsideration of the idea of the individual producer or consumer of culture – even as corporate content 'owners' continue, in varying degrees, to assert rights that have their basis in the romantic notion of the individual creative author (Herman et al., 2006). It is not only the 'who' of production that is transformed in contemporary digital culture, but the *how*. (pp. 7–8)

Furthermore, Burgess details three important structural transformations from the point of view of cultural participation implied by the Web 2.0 model. I summarize from Burgess as follows:

1. The shift from content "production," "distribution" and "consumption" to a convergence of all three, resulting in a hybrid mode of engagement called "produsage," defined as "the collaborative and continuous building and extending of existing content in pursuit of further improvement" (Bruns, 2005).
2. A shift from "user-generated content" to "user-led" content creation, editing, repurposing, and distribution; whereby the users of a given Web service increasingly take on leadership roles, and where designers and developers to some extent allow the emergence of communities of practice to shape the culture of the network – even to determine what the Web service or online community is "for." This dynamic represents a convergence of the "value chain" where users are simultaneously the producers, users, editors and consumers of the content, leading to "network effects."

3. The convergence of user-generated content and social software to produce hybrid spaces, examples of which are sometimes described as "social media" (Coates, 2006) – most clearly represented by MySpace, YouTube and Flickr (Burgess, 2007, pp. 10–11)

Burgess (2007) argues:

It is this third feature of the new networks of cultural production that has the most profound implications for cultural participation, at least in potential, because this shift opens up new and diverse spaces for individuals to engage with a variety of aesthetic experiences at the same time as their participation contributes to the creation of communities. That is, the significance of "Web 2.0," from a cultural studies point of view, lies in its potential for a new configuration of the relations between the *aesthetic* and the *social* aspects of culture, developed at a grass-roots level. (p. 11)

As many scholars and commentators have suggested since the "change merchants" of the 1970s – Marshall McLuhan, Drucker, and Alvin Toffler – first raised the issue we are in the middle of a long-term cultural evolutionary shift based on the digitization and the logic of open systems that has the capacity to profoundly change all aspects of our daily lives – work, home, school – and existing systems of culture and economy. A wide range of scholars from different disciplines and new media organizations have speculated on the nature of the shift: Richard Stallman established the Free Software Movement and the GNU project[5]; Yochai Benkler (2006), the Yale law professor, has commented on the wealth of networks and the way that social production transforms freedom and markets; his colleague, Larry Lessig (2004, 2007), also a law professor, has written convincingly on code, copyright, and the creative commons[6] and launched the Free Culture Movement designed to promote the freedom to distribute and modify creative works through the new social media[7]; Students for Free Culture,[8] launched in 2004, "is a diverse, non-partisan group of students and young people who are working to get their peers involved in the free culture movement"; Michel Bauwens (2005) has written about the political economy of peer production and established the P-2-P Foundation[9]; Creative Commons[10] was founded in 2001 by experts in cyber law and intellectual property; Wikipedia[11] the world's largest and open-content encyclopedia was established in 2001 by Jimmy Wales, an American Internet entrepreneur, whose blog is subtitled Free Knowledge for Free Minds.[12]

One influential definition suggests

Social and technological advances make it possible for a growing part of humanity to *access, create, modify, publish and distribute* various kinds of works – artworks, scientific and educational materials, software, articles – in short: *anything that can be represented in digital form.* Many communities have formed to exercise those new possibilities and create a wealth of collectively re-usable works.

CHAPTER 2

By *freedom* they mean:

- the *freedom to use* the work and enjoy the benefits of using it
- the *freedom to study* the work and to apply knowledge acquired from it
- the *freedom to make and redistribute copies*, in whole or in part, of the information or expression
- the *freedom to make changes and improvements*, and to distribute derivative works.[13]

This is how the Open Cultures Working Group – an open group of artists, researchers and cultural activists – describe the situation in their Vienna Document subtitled *Xnational Net Culture and "The Need to Know" of Information Societies:*

> Information technologies are setting the global stage for economic and cultural change. More than ever, involvement in shaping the future calls for a wide understanding and reflection on the ecology and politics of information cultures. So called globalization not only signifies a worldwide network of exchange but new forms of hierarchies and fragmentation, producing deep transformations in both physical spaces and immaterial information domains... global communication technologies still hold a significant potential for empowerment, cultural expression and transnational collaboration. To fully realize the potential of life in global information societies we need to acknowledge the plurality of agents in the information landscape and the heterogeneity of collaborative cultural practice. The exploration of alternative futures is linked to a living cultural commons and social practice based on networks of open exchange and communication.[14]

Every aspect of culture and economy is becoming transformed through the process of digitization that creates new systems of archives, representation, and reproduction technologies that portend Web 3.0 and Web 4.0 where all production, material and immaterial, is digitally designed and coordinated through distributed information systems. As Felix Staler (2004) remarks "information can be infinitely copied, easily distributed, and endlessly transformed. Contrary to analog culture, other people's work is not just referenced, but directly incorporated through copying and pasting, remixing, and other standard digital procedures." Digitization transforms all aspects of cultural production and consumption favoring the networked peer community over the individual author and blurring the distinction between artists and their audiences. These new digital logics alter the logic of the organization of knowledge, education, and culture spawning new technologies as a condition of the openness of the system. Now the production of texts, sounds, and images is open to new rounds of experimentation and development providing what Staler calls "a new grammar of digital culture." Furthermore, the processes of creativity are no longer controlled by traditional knowledge institutions and organizations but rather have emerged as platforms and infrastructures that encourage large-scale participation and challenge old hierarchies.

The shift to networked media cultures based on the ethics of participation, sharing, and collaboration, involving a volunteer, peer-to-peer gift economy has its early beginnings in the right to freedom of speech that depended upon the flow and exchange of ideas essential to political democracy, including the notion of a "free press," the market and the academy. Perhaps, even more fundamentally free speech is a significant personal, psychological, and educational good that promotes self-expression and creativity and also the autonomy and development of the self necessary for representation in a linguistic and political sense and the formation of identity.

NOTES

[1] This chapter draws on my Introduction to *Creativity in the Global Knowledge Economy* (Peters, Marginson & Murphy, 2009).

[2] These statements are taken from the New Club of Rome's 2006 Manifesto at http://www.the-new-club-of-paris.org/mission.htm.

[3] See The Center for Accelerated learning at http://www.alcenter.com/; see e.g., The Framework for Gifted Education at http://education.qld.gov.au/ publication/production/reports/pdfs/giftedandtalfwrk. pdf.

[4] For innovation theory see the Swedish economist Bengt-Åke Lundvall's Web page at http://www.business.aau.dk/ike/members/bal.html and especially his concept of "the learning economy"; see also Globelics, The Global Network for the Economics of Learning, Innovation, and Competence Building Systems at http://www.globelics.org/.

[5] See the GNU site http://www.gnu.org/gnu/initial-announcement.html, a 2006 lecture by Stallman entitled "The Free Software Movement and the Future of Freedom" and Aaron Renn's (1998) "Free," "Open Source," and Philosophies of Software Ownership at http://www.urbanophile.com/ arenn/ hacking/fsvos.html.

[6] See his bestseller *Free Culture* http://www.free-culture.cc/freeculture.pdf.

[7] See the videoblog "Free Culture, Free Software, Free Infrastructures! Openness and Freedom in every Layer of the Network" at http://www. perspektive89.com/2006/10/18/free_culture_free_ software_free_infrastructures_openness_and_freedom_in_every_layer_of_the_network_flo_fleissig_ episo but see also Pasquinelli's (2008) "The Ideology of Free Culture and the Grammar of Sabotage" at http://www.rekombinant.org/docs/Ideology-of-Free-Culture.pdf.

[8] See the Web site http://freeculture.org/.

[9] See the foundation at http://p2pfoundation.net/The_Foundation_for_P2P_Alternativesandthe associated blog at http://blog.p2pfoundation.net/.

[10] See http://creativecommons.org/.

[11] See http://www.wikipedia.org/.

[12] See http://blog.jimmywales.com/.

[13] See http://freedomdefined.org/Definition.

[14] See http://world-information.org/wio/readme/992003309/11343967 02.

REFERENCES

Aitken H. J. (2004). "Measure Intelligence, Achievement, Openness to Experience and Creativity," *Personality & Individual Differences, 36*(4): 913–930.

Banks, J. (2002). Gamers as Co-Creators: Enlisting the Virtual Audience – a Report From the Net Face. In M. Balnaves, T. O'Regan & J. Sternberg (Eds.). *Mobilising the Audience*. Brisbane: University of Queensland Press.

Baumol, W. J. (2002). *The Free-market Innovation Machine: Analyzing the Growth Miracle of Capitalism*. Princeton, NJ: Princeton University Press.

Bell, D. (1973). The coming of post-industrial society: A venture in social forecasting. New York: Basic Books.

Benkler, Y. (2006). *The Wealth of Networks*. New Haven, CT: Yale University Press.

Bentley, T. & Wilsdon, J. (Eds.) (2003). *The Adaptive State – Strategies for Personalising the Public Realm*. London: Demos. Retrieved from http://www.demos.co.uk/files/HPAPft.pdf.

Blythe, M. (2000). *Creative Learning Futures: Literature Review of Training and Development Needs in the Creative Industries*. Retrieved from http://www.cadise.ac.uk/projects/creativelearning/New_Lit.doc.

Brown, J. S. & Duguid, P. (2000). *The Social Life of Information*. Boston: Harvard Business School Press.

Bruns, A. (2005). Anyone Can Edit: Understanding the Produser. *The Mojtaba Saminejad Lecture*.

Burgess, J. (2007). *Vernacular Creativity and the New Media*. Doctoral dissertation, Creative Industries Faculty, Queensland University of Technology). Retrieved from http://eprints.qut.edu.au/10076/1/Burgess_PhD_FINAL.pdf

Caves, R. E. (2000). *Creative Industries: Contracts between Art and Commerce*. Cambridge, MA: Harvard University Press.

Chesbrough, Henry (2001). "The Intel Lookout", MIT Technology Review, October 9, 2001.

Chesbrough, Henry (2001). "Old Dogs Can Learn New Tricks", MIT Technology Review, July 18, 2001.

Chesbrough, Henry (2001). "Is the Central R&D Lab Obsolete?", MIT Technology Review, April 24, 2001.

Coates, T. (2006). What do we do with "Social media"? Retrieved from http://www.plasticbag.org/archives/2006/03/what_do_we_do_with_social_media.shtml

Cowen, T. (2002). *Creative Destruction: How Globalization Is Changing the World's Cultures*. Princeton, NJ: Princeton University Press.

Davenport, T. & Beck, J. (2001). *The Attention Economy: Understanding the New Economy of Business*. Cambridge, MA: Harvard Business School Press.

Davis, J., Stack, M. (1997). The digital Advantage. In: Davis, J., Hirschl, T., Stack, M. (Eds.), *The Cutting Edge, Technology, Information, Capitalism and Social Revolution*. London: Verso, pp. 121–144.

Dollinger, S. J. (2007). "Creativity and Conservatism," *Personality & Individual Differences, 43*(5): 1025–1035.

Fischer, G. & Giaccardi, E. (2007). "Sustaining Social Creativity," *Communications of the ACM, 50*(12).

Florida, R. (2002). *The Rise of the Creative Class*. New York: Basic Books.

Foray, D. (2004). *The Economics of Knowledge*. Cambridge, MA: MIT Press.

Frey, B. (2000). Arts and Economics: Analysis and Cultural Policy. New York: Springer.

Frey, B. S. & Pommerehne, W. W. (1989). *Muses and Markets: Explorations in the Economics of the Arts*. Cambridge, MA: Blackwell.

Fuller, J., Jawecki, G. & Muhlbacher, H. (2007). "Innovation Creation by Online Basketball Communities," *Journal of Business Research, 60*(1): 60–71.

Ginsburgh, Victor A. & Menger, P.-M. (Eds.) (1996). *Economics of the Arts*. Amsterdam: North Holland.

Goldman, R. & Gabriel, R. P. (2005). *Innovation Happens Elsewhere: Open Source as Business Strategy*. San Francisco: Morgan Kaufmann.

Gordon, W. J. (1993). "A Property Right in Self-expression: Equality and Individualism in the Natural Law of Intellectual Property," 102 *Yale Law Journal 1533*: 1568–1572.

Heilbrun, J. & Gray, C. M. (2001). *The Economics of Art and Culture*, 2nd ed. New York: Cambridge University Press.

Herman, A., Coombe, R.J. & Kaye, L. (2006). Your Second Life? Goodwill and the Performativity of Intellectual Property in Online Gaming, *Cultural Studies, 20*(2–3): 184–210.

Hesmondhalgh, D. (2002). *The Cultural Industries*. Thousand Oaks, CA: Sage.

Hippel, E.V. (1988). *The sources of innovation*. Oxford: Oxford University Press.

Howkins, J. (2001). *The Creative Economy: How People Make Money from Ideas*. London: Allen Lane.

Hughes, J. (1988). "The Philosophy of Intellectual Property," 77 *Georgetown Law Journal 287*: 337–344.

Humphreys, S. (2005). Productive Players: Online Computer Games' Challenge to Conventional Media Forms, *Journal of Communication and Critical/Cultural Studies, 2*(1): 36–50.

Johnson, C. (2005). *Varieties of openness in evolutionary creativity.* Retrieved from http://kar.kent.ac. uk/14358/1/VarietiesColin.pdf.

Jones, P. (2001). "Open(source)ing the Doors for Contributor-run Digital Libraries," *Communications of the Association for Computing Machinery, 44*(5): 45–46. Retrieved from http://delivery.acm.org/ 10.1145/380000/374337/p45-jones.html?key1=374337&key2= 9102569901& coll=ACM&dl= ACM& CFID=11722369&CFTOKEN=18823426.

Karaganis, J. (Ed.) (2008). *Structures of Participation in Digital Culture.* New York: Columbia University Press.

Keats, D. (2003). "Collaborative Development of Open Content: A Process Model to Unlock the Potential for African Universities," *First Monday, 8*(3): Retrieved from http://firstmonday.org/issues/ issue8_2/keats/ index.html.

Kelly K. (1998). *New Rules for the New Economy.* London: Fourth Estate.

Landry, C. (2000). *The Creative City: A Toolkit for Urban Innovators.* London: Earthscan.

Lash, S. & Urry, J. (1994). *Economies of Signs and Space.* Thousand Oaks, CA: Sage.

Leadbeater, C. (2003.), "Open Innovation in Public Services," *The Adaptive State – Strategies for Personalising the Public Realm.* T. Bentley and J. Wilsdon (Eds.), *Demos*: 37–49. Retrieved from http://www.demos.co. uk/files/HPAPft.pdf.

Lemley, M. A. (2005). "Property, Intellectual Property, and Free Riding," 83 *Texas Law Review* 1031, 1031.

Lessig, L. (2006). *Code: Version 2.0.* New York: Basic Books.

Morris-Suzuki, T. (1997). "Capitalism in the Computer Age and Afterward," in J. Davis, T. A. Hirschl, & M. Stack (Eds.), *Cutting Edge: Technology, Information Capitalism and Social Revolution.* London: Verso, 57–72.

Mulgan, G. (2005). "A Wiki Way to Work and Spread Scholarship," *The Times Higher Education Supplement,* 12.

Mulgan, G., Salem, O. & Steinberg, T. (2005). *Wide Open: Open Source Methods and Their Future.* London: Demos. Retrieved from http:// www.demos.co.uk/catalogue/wideopen/.

National Academy of Sciences (2003). *Beyond Productivity: Information Technology, Innovation and Creativity.* Washington, DC: NAS Press.

Netanel, N. W. (1996). "Copyright and a Democratic Civil Society," 106 *Yale Law Journal 283*: 347–362.

Netanel, N. W. (1998). "Asserting Copyright's Democratic Principles in the Global Arena," 51 *Vanderbilt Law Review 217*: 272–276.

Peters, M.A. (2009). Education, creativity, and the economy of passion. In M.A. Peters, S. Marginson, and P. Murphy (Eds.). *Creativity, and the global knowledge economy,* pp. 125–148. London and New York: Peter Lang.

Peters, M.A. (2010). Introduction: Knowledge goods, the primacy of ideas and the economics of abundance. In M.A. Peters, S. Marginson, and P. Murphy (Eds.). *Creativity, and the global knowledge economy,* pp. 1–22. London and New York: Peter Lang.

Prabhu, V., Sutton, C. & Sauser, W. (2008). "Creativity and Certain Personality Traits: Understanding the Mediating Effect of Intrinsic Motivation," *Creativity Research Journal, 20*(1): 53–66.

Rutten, R. & Gelissen, J. (2008). "Technology, Talent, Diversity and the Wealth of European Regions," *European Planning Studies, 16*(7).

Schweik, C., Evans, T. & Grove, J. M. (2005). "Open Source and Open Content: A Framework for Global Collaboration in Social-ecological Research," *Ecology and Society, 10*(1). Retrieved from http://www.ecology andsociety.org/vol10/iss1/.

Shapiro, C. & Varian, H. (1998). *Information Rules: A Strategic Guide to the Network Economy.* Cambridge, MA: Harvard Business School Press.

Shapiro, C. & Varian, H.R. (1998). *Information rules: A strategic guide to the network economy.* Boston, MA: Harvard Business School Press.

Shneiderman, B. (2007). "Creativity Support Tools," *Communications of the ACM, 50*(12).

Simonton, D. K. (2000). "Creativity: Cognitive, Personal, Developmental, and Social Aspects," *American Psychologist, 55*(1): 151–158.

Stalder, F. (2004). Open Cultures and the Nature of Networks. Retrieved from: http://felix.openflows. com/pdf/Notebook_eng.pdf

Stiglitz, J. (1999a). "Knowledge as a global public good," Retrieved from http://www.worldbank. org/knowledge/chiefecon/articles/undpk2/ (accessed 30 August, 2008).

Stiglitz, J. E. (1999b). "Knowledge as a Global Public Good," *Global Public Goods 19*: 308–326.

Surowiecki, J. (2004). *The Wisdom of Crowds: Why the Many Are Smarter than the Few and How Collective Wisdom Shapes Business, Economies, Societies and Nations.* New York: Anchor.

Tapscott, D. & Williams, A. D. (2006). *Wikinomics: How Mass Collaboration Changes Everything.* New York: Atlantic Books.

Teirlinck, P. & Spithoven, A. (2008). "The Spatial Organization of Innovation: Open Innovation, External Knowledge Relations and Urban Structure," *Regional Studies, 42*(5): 689–704.

Tippett, J. (2007). "Creativity, Networks and Openness – The Potential Value of an Open Source Approach to Support Practitioners in Planning for Sustainability," Retrieved from http://www .aesop2007napoli.it/full_paper/ track3/track3_298.pdf.

Toffler, A. (1980). *The Third Wave.* New York: Bantam Books.

Touraine, A. (1971). *The Post-industrial Society: Tomorrow's Social History: Classes Conflicts and Culture in the Programmed Society.* L. Mayhew (trans.). New York: Random House.

Varian, H.R., Rabasco, M.E. & Toharia, L. (1998). *Microeconomía intermedia: un enfoque actual.* Barcelona: Antoni Bosch.

Verschraegen, G. & Schiltz, M. (2007). "Knowledge as a Global Public Good: The Role and Importance of Open Access," *Societies without Borders, 2*(2): 157–174.

Wagner, R. P. (2003). "Information Wants to Be Free: Intellectual Property and the Mythologies of Control," 103 *Columbia Law Review 995*: 1001–1003.

Weber, S. (2004). *The Success of Open Source.* Cambridge, MA: Harvard University Press.

CHAPTER 3

ESOTERIC AND OPEN PEDAGOGIES

INTRODUCTION

The developments of new technologies and open resources within society have fostered the new creation of different pedagogies including what we call Open Learning Systems (OLS). This article examines the shift from *esoteric* to *open* pedagogy and the consequent changes for education and knowledge creation. Traditionally, creative and 'free' thinking was confined to esoteric pedagogical traditions for reasons to do with persecution and censorship. Even today many education systems are not open in the sense that they may still be exclusive due to limited access and resources. This article examines the traditions of esoteric and open pedagogy in an historical light. With a focus on openness, concepts in open pedagogy in modern era provide new perspectives for education systems. Developments of new technologies and open resources have fostered new forms of pedagogy. In particular, the creation and understanding of (OLS) pedagogy will provide insight into learning within new electronic environments. Within the new forms of open pedagogy (OLS) scholars, teachers, students, and the public can flourish in actively participating and collaborating in all phases of knowledge creation.

Education has changed from esoteric pedagogical traditions toward open education through the development of new information and communications infrastructures that enable P2P architectures and encourage a new ethic of collaboration and sharing. As these new forms of technology and open resources develop so too do the scope and structure of open pedagogies. Information has always been central to the democratic form of life and it has begun to reshape and reconfigure the public realm and the institutional of democracy itself. Following the democratic movement globally and internet development, education has been quick to embrace these new concepts of openness and to develop novel systems of access, archiving, educational resources and course management that help to promote it. These open conditions and ideas lead to the need of open pedagogies. Open pedagogies are characterized by several important aspects, including the ideology of openness in its philosophic, social and psychological aspects, the provision of open educational resources, and open teaching and learning conditions. In addition, open pedagogies has already changed the learning environment and will have profound effects in the emergence of global education systems. Open pedagogy provides opportunities for inclusive learning and collective knowledge production. These historical changes differ from esoteric pedagogical tradition. We provide a brief discussion of the ideologies of secrecy and openness within the context of Western philosophy with a focus on 'hidden codes' of modernity (that which remains hidden to us but governs our behavior) and be reference to the what Lyotard (1984) calls the 'crisis of narratives'. We also provide a brief discussion of the tradition of esoteric pedagogy by reference to the work of Leo Strauss before taking up the issue of closed/secret society vs open/democratic society. In the final section we discuss the philosophy of open pedagogy in terms of a series of characterisitics.

IDEOLOGIES OF OPENNESS & SECRECY

One of the most enduring and seductive ideologies of the twentieth century and a central aspect of modernism is the idea that *something lies hidden from us*—truth, knowledge, reality – and that which lies hidden yet governs us, our thinking or behavior. The other central part of this idea is that with the right tools of analysis or methodology what is hidden can be exposed or brought to the surface and its true form be known. This central trope is very dominant not only in the forms of logicism inaugurated by Frege, Russell and Wittgenstein and in the various strands of structuralism going back at least to Ferdinand de Saussure, Pierce, and Jacobson but also in development of European formalism per se. One could argue that the lineage of such an idea can be traced all the way back to Plato and to his idea of the world of forms – abstract entities that exist independently of the sensible world— and his distinction between the world of appearances and the world of forms.[1] While it has persisted in one form or another since Plato (and perhaps even earlier), it takes on a distinctive ethos in the twentieth century and comes close to defining a central aspect of modernism.[2]

We call this idea an *ideology* and use the word 'ideology' in this context in the original sense coined by Destutt de Tracy, the French Enlightenment thinker, in his massive work *Éléments d'idéologie* (1801–1815). He coined the term in 1796 to refer to a 'science of the formation of ideas', a kind of superscience which replaced theology. He was strongly influenced by Locke and Condillac and was characterized by deductive methods applied especially to concepts of private property. He believed with Locke that that much of reality could not be reduced to mathematical constructs (hence the connection to both formalism and modernism; and, one might argue, also liberalism[3]). We use Tracy's concept more in the sense that Jean-François Lyotard (1984) uses the term 'metanarrative', especially in *The Postmodern Condition*, where he talks of 'incredulity towards metanarratives' to characterize the skepticism that now typifies our outlook where he is referring to the 'grand narratives' that define modernity.

The Postmodern Condition developed a philosophical interpretation of the changing state of knowledge, science and education in the most highly developed societies, reviewing and synthesizing research on contemporary science within the broader context of the sociology of postindustrial society and studies of postmodern culture. Lyotard brought together for the first time diverse threads and previously separate literatures in an analysis which many commentators and critics believed to signal an epochal break not only with the so-called 'modern era' but also with various traditionally 'modern' ways of viewing the world. Lyotard's major working hypothesis: 'that the status of knowledge is altered as societies enter what is known as the postindustrial age and cultures enter what is known as the postmodern age' (1984: 3). He uses the term 'postmodern condition' to describe the state of knowledge and the problem of its legitimation in the most highly developed societies. In this he follows sociologists and critics who have used the term to designate the state of Western culture 'following the transformations which, since the end of the nineteenth century, have altered the game rules for science, literaure and the arts' (Lyotard, 1984: 3). Lyotard places these transformations within the context of the *crisis of narratives*, especially those Enlightenment metanarratives concerning 'meaning', 'truth' and 'emancipation' which have been used to legitimate both the rules of knowledge of the sciences and the foundations of modern institutions.

In one sense, therefore, Lyotard is drawing our attention to these grand narratives and I want to restrict the term 'ideologies of knowledge' to narratives concerning knowledge and truth. In the twentieth century the notion that knowledge or truth is hidden from us is clearly illustrated in the works of Marx, Freud, Breton, and Wittgenstein, to name a few of the most obvious examples. Marx & Engels (1970: 46–7) uses the term 'ideology' to generally imply a false sense of consciousness stated in the following form: 'the life process of ... individuals, ... as they may appear in their own or other people's imagination, – – . what men say, imagine, conceive ... men as narrated, thought of, imagine, conceived, ...' on the model that 'Life is not determined by consciousness, but consciousness by life.' Marxist radical political economy and analysis of class relations are the tools that reveal true social reality.

The same general model is followed by Freud. In this case the Unconscious is that which needs revealing and the true coordinates that govern behavior are located in that dark region of the unconscious mind which harbors wishes and desires, traumas and painful memories that have been repressed. The unconscious is a force that only reveals itself as a symptom. Freud employed different models of the unconscious. His early topographical or spatial model (preconscious, conscious unconscious) was characterized by the will as a set of drives operating behind the conscious mind. In another more dynamic model Freud divides the unconscious into the Id, an instinctual part, and the Superego, a kind of conscience. Freud's followers, notably Jung who invented the concept of the collective unconscious, and Lacan, who maintained that the unconscious is structured like a language, employed different models that have strong implications for analysis and the tools used to get at the unconscious. Psychoanalysis was the set of techniques including interpretation of dreams and transference and resistance analysis of associations constitute the tools for analysis to reveal the true psychic reality.

Strongly influenced by both Marx and Freud, Andre Breton in his *Manifesto of Surrealism* (1924) defined surrealism as 'pure psychic automatism, by which an attempt is made to express, either verbally, in writing or in any other manner, the true functioning of thought. The dictation of thought, in the absence of all control by reason, excluding any aesthetic or moral preoccupation.' In his essay 'What is Surrealism?' Breton (1934) writes:

A certain immediate ambiguity contained in the word *surrealism*, is, in fact, capable of leading one to suppose that it designates I know not what transcendental attitude, while, on the contrary it expresses—and always has expressed for us—a desire to deepen the foundations of the real, to bring about an even clearer and at the same time ever more passionate consciousness of the world perceived by the senses. The whole evolution of surrealism, from its origins to the present day, which I am about to retrace, shows that our unceasing wish, growing more and more urgent from day to day, has been at all costs to avoid considering a system of thought as a refuge, to pursue our investigations with eyes wide open to their outside consequences, and to assure ourselves that the results of these investigations would be capable of facing the *breath of the street*. At the limits, for many years past—or more exactly, since the conclusion of what one may term the purely *intuitive* epoch of surrealism (1919–25)—at the limits, I say, we have attempted to present interior reality and exterior reality as two elements in process of unification, or finally becoming *one*. This final unification is the supreme aim of surrealism: interior reality and exterior reality being, in the present form of society, in contradiction (and in this contradiction we see the very cause of man's unhappiness, but also the source of his movement), we have assigned to ourselves the task of confronting these two realities with one another on every possible occasion, of refusing to allow the preeminence of the one over the other, yet not of acting on the one and on the other *both at once*, for that would be to suppose that they are less apart from one another than they are (and I believe that those who pretend that they are acting on both simultaneously are either deceiving us or are a prey to a disquieting illusion); of acting on these two realities not both at once, then, but one after the other, in a systematic manner, allowing us to observe their reciprocal attraction and interpenetration and to give to this interplay of forces all the extension necessary for the trend of these two adjoining realities to become one and the same thing.

In this extract we can see clearly the modernist trope clearly at work: to reveal the formal structure of that which is hidden.

In the early Wittgenstein we have a similar proposal although for Wittgenstein the quarry is the logical form of a sentence that depicts or is capable of depicting the world. The main tenants of Wittgenstein logical atomism is given as follows:

Every proposition has a unique final analysis which reveals it to be a truth-function of elementary propositions asserting the existence of atomic states of affairs (*Tractatus* 3.25, 4.21, 4.221, 5); (ii) Elementary propositions are mutually independent—each one can be true or false independently of the truth or falsity of the others (4.211, 5.134); (iii) Elementary propositions are immediate combinations of semantically simple symbols or "names" (4.221); (iv) Names refer to items wholly devoid of complexity, so-called "objects" (2.02 & 3.22); (v) Atomic states of affairs are combinations of these simple objects (2.01) (http://plato.stanford.edu/entries/wittgenstein-atomism/).

Wittgenstein aims at 'complete analysis' and complete clarity on the understanding that language and the world share a basic logical structure or form which can be revealed through analysis.

These are all examples of the notion of deep structure, of that which is hidden from us that governs our behavior or understanding and the aim of method is to unthread, expose, or make manifest that which is hidden. Such an ideology also operates strongly in various models of the text and of criticism that is evident in forms of scriptural interpretation, hermeneutics, and textual criticism. In this case the forms of textual and literary criticism provide the means by which to unlock the secrets of the text, its deeper meaning, especially when these are obviously allegorical, fable-ized, or metaphorical. In model of classical texts reference is made to both internal (style, vocabulary, immediate context, manuscript tradition or stemma etc.) and external (witnesses, genealogies of families of texts etc) evidence to produce authoritative readings. In the case of Marxist tradition of literary criticism where a modified form of the base/superstructure model looms large in the work of Lukacs, Gramsci and Althusser and ideology has become important in contemporary theorists like Raymond Williams and Terry Eagleton the application is easy to observe. Literary theory, from the moment Plato's expressed skepticism about signification and the lack of an etymological relationship between words and meanings to its emergence in German philological studies and its institutionalization in the twentieth century, the emphasis has been on the development and refinement of a set of tools of analysis that will release the meanings of a text through a form of critical practice.

ESOTERIC PEDAGOGY

There is an older tradition that employs the same modernist trope which we can call the tradition of *esoteric knowledge* that has been revitalized and brought to the fore in political philosophy by Leo Strauss. His work not only makes esoteric knowledge central to political philosophy but it also makes it central to pedagogy.

Leo Strauss, a German-Jewish émigré, was a student of Ernst Cassirer at the University of Hamburg (completing his doctorate on Jacobi in 1924), attended lectures by both Husserl and Heidegger, and who was colleagues with some of the most prominent German intellectuals of the 1920s and '30s including, Jacob Klein, Karl Löwith, Gerard Krüger, Juilius Guttman, Hans-Georg Gadamer, Franz Rosenzweig, Gershom Scholem, Alexander Altmann and Paul Kraus. In 1932 Strauss left Germany on a Rockefeller scholarship traveling first to Paris where he became a close friend of Alexandre Kojeve, then to England where he became friendly with Tawney at Cambridge, before immigrating to the United States in 1937 to work at the New School for Social Research (called 'the University in Exile') between 1938–48. He became of US citizen in 1944 and accepted a position as professor of political science at the University of Chicago in 1949, a position he held until 1968.

Strauss was responsible for bringing the question of modernity to the US—what he called 'the theological-philosophical problem'– and making it central to political philosophy and, indeed, as some contemporary scholars, central to US neo-conservatism. He published *Persecution and the Art of Writing* in 1952 where he argued that philosophers engaged in a tradition of esoteric writing to avoid persecution by the State or Church while at the same time communicating with a select audience who with proper education could come to know the secret or coded meanings of the ancient texts. Strauss maintained that philosophers offer both an exoteric or salutary teaching and an esoteric or true teaching which was concealed from the general reader. In order to understand this esoteric reading of Strauss better it is useful and productive to briefly examine the tradition of esoteric knowledge.

In the contemporary West, it is hard to understand nowadays that attitudes to knowledge and especially to public knowledge, including a historically developed set of rights to free speech, inquiry and publication and universal access to knowledge have not always existed. Indeed, whether these rights and the universal ethos on which they are based exist today is a matter for ongoing debate. Some would argue that we are currently undergoing a gigantic shift in the political economy of knowledge coinciding with the 'knowledge economy' that encourages a shift to the wholesale privatization and private ownership of knowledge against the history of liberalism. Whether this is the case or not, whether these liberal freedoms concerning knowledge are being transformed and reprivatized or not, it is the case that attitudes and rights to knowledge were never as liberal as they were during the era of the welfare state and especially in the period immediately after WWII leading up to the time when liberal democracies during the 1970s and after set up legislation that was variously called the official information act or official secrets act, the purpose of which was to spell out in law the safeguarding of information, authorized disclosures and decision procedures for the release of official information (often under the auspices of an ombudsman).

The tradition of esoteric knowledge is not a single tradition but rather comprised of many threads that took different forms and often involved the development of secret societies with special initiation rituals. Esotericism is often associated with the growth of mystery religions that developed after Christianity became the official religion of the Roman Empire. Many dissident groups developed and these were associated not only with mysticism but also with privileged access and ways of reading the sacred texts. Thus, for instance, Gnosticism, derived from the Greek *gnostikos* (one who has *gnosis*, or 'secret knowledge'), emphasized a form of secret knowledge through revelation and 'gospels' that was opposed and denied by the Church Fathers. Some scholars have argued that the Gnostics predate Christianity and have their origins in pre-Christian religions, such as the Pythagorian Platonists including Figulus and Eudorus of Alexandria.[4] The term *esoteric* first appeared in Thomas Stanley's *History of Philosophy* (1701) where describing the 'auditors of Pythagoras' he indicated that Pythagoreans were divided into exoteric, those under review, and esoteric, those who had been admitted into the inner circle.

The Gnostic writings themselves, early Christian literature[5] including The Gospel of St Thomas, The Secret Book of James, Acts of Peter, Acts of Thomas, Gospel of Truth and the recently famous Gospel of Judas, an ancient Coptic manuscript of the 3rd or 4th century and only surviving copy of the gospel recently restored and authenticated by a team of scholars from National Geographical

Society with the Maecenas Foundation for Ancient Art and the Waitt Institute for Historical Discovery,[6] display a diversity in theology and Christian sects that defy the Church canon and institution.

The tradition of esoteric knowledge is also caught up in the origins and methodological refinements of hermeneutics as an approach to the study, translation and interpretation of texts. It sources can be traced back to the ancient study of rhetoric by the Greeks on the one hand and traditions of biblical hermeneutics and exegesis, on the other. Rhetoric is as old as the pre-Socratics Sophists, the wandering or itinerant teacher-philosophers like Protagoras, who offered advice and offered persuasive arguments. It later became part of the medieval liberal arts curriculum along with logic and dialectics, comprised of the study of grammar and style. Biblical exegesis took a variety of forms. *Midrash* is the Hebrew word referring to a method of exegesis where interpretation, especially in the Pardes system, makes distinctions between *peshat* (simple), *remez* (hints or clues), *derash* (interpretation) and *sod* (mystical or secret) meanings of biblical verse. The term Midrash can also refer to teachings that take the form of legal, exegetical or homilectic commentaries on the *Tanakh*. It was essential in these textual investigations as in Plato's, utilizing various philological tools and forms of analysis, to distinguish between literal and allegorical readings, between literal and deeper meaning of the text. The Patristics distinguished between the literal sense (*sensus historicus*), what Scripture says directly, the allegorical sense (*sensus allegoricus*)that elucidates the Church's doctrinal content by providing a symbolic meaning for each literal element. Both these are separate from the moral meanings or teachings to be derived from the Scripture (*sensus tropologicus* or *sensus moralis*) and, finally, the *sensus anagogicus*, the implicit allusions to secret metaphysical and eschatological knowledge (*gnosis*). These various techniques of medieval hermeneutics were used by both the early Jewish Rabbis and early Church Fathers to gain access to the deeper meanings of the text that lay hidden below the surface or literal meanings.

Secret societies[7] such as the Free Thinkers, the Freemasons, and many of the fraternities and sonorities that have grown up on American campuses, swear their members to secrecy and have secret initiation ceremonies.

CLOSED/SECRET VS. OPEN/DEMOCRATIC

The knowledge system from esoteric to open took much time to develop. The dilemma of whether knowledge should be preserved for literacy people or public resulted from limited resource and technology development. In the early age, most education only provided to elite class. As society developed into modern and democratic form, education became more inclusive to the public.

Esoteric System

Education and learning were limited to elite class in the beginning of human history. The limited transportation in accent time provided homogeneous society and religion played important role. Only those who served religion work or upper class were able to learn. The exclusive learning environment often contained all kinds of 'initiations' that characterized occupational initiation which included obeying secrets and codes that esoteric knowledge.

Later on, as civilization developed, education was remained limited in society. For examples, in Egypt, learning hieroglyph was limited for scribes, the Sumerians (who used cuneiform) and Phoenicians (who developed alphabets) were hard to indentify where they learned but possible indicated that not all people were able to learn. The Hebrews had Synagogue for learning their religion and meeting for all. In Greek city-states, only the liberated citizens were able to learn. Knowledge learning remained as limited and closed to selected people.

In the middle age, parish system started to educate local presents and mostly on Christian meaning and Catechism. Charles the Great conducted 'Carolingian Renaissance' that encouraged education activities. In addition, Alfred the Great in England also encouraged education and using Anglo-Saxon language. However, their efforts were not pay out after their death. Learning knowledge remained in esoteric form. Even later on, began the Feudal society that had Chivalry education and started Gild that involved apprenticeship learning and foundation of Universities. These learning was restricted only to selected people and remained more of secret and esoteric to others. Some science society also remained close to the public to avoid Church's anti-scientific repressed that limited knowledge into secret private field.

Around 16 century, St. Ignatius of Loyola established 'Jesuit' and had over hundreds of schools to provide education for many (Cubberley, 1920). In addition, Jean Baptiste de la Salla created 'Christian Brother' to provide basic education mostly for lower class people (Compayré, 1900). Johann Heinrich Pestalozzi had orphan asylum and focused on educating the youths and shifted education interest from adults to children (Compayré, 1900, Monroe, 1970).

Additionally, in Asian area, such as China, education learning was also limited to a certain population. Mostly were those officers and who were studying for attending governor positions might get their education. In general population, under Confucianism influenced, some literacy people conducted some basic learning school for general people. However, these schools were more of basic literacy for daily living and not for knowledge developing and creating. The form of education was more of teacher-based one-way instruction instead of cooperative knowledge creation and open to knowledge construction.

In broad history perspective, education was in the close condition that focused on teaching a few people and limited to certain knowledge. The teaching style also restricted as one-way instruction and limited forms. Knowledge system was exclusive (to the public aspect) and close to others. This did not change until new public school system was established. Additionally, the open and interactive teaching-learning environment is still prestige to only some education system globally.

Open Knowledge System

Some period of time in limited area there was some general education introduced to most civilians. However, it was until religion revolution that reform churches encouraged people to be able to read Bible and the Vatican fought back to equipped followers with literacy that gave the public chances to learn. These teaching and learning did not directly relate to knowledge creation. Knowledge was restricted and controlled by authority and mostly in the hands of church, government and a few distinguished people. It was not until starting of more democratic society that gave more people to involve in knowledge creation. As what Foucault critiqued on knowledge and power relationship, knowledge was defined and controlled by limited authorities.

In democratic society, when society started to open opportunities to the public that more people could learn and attend knowledge production would lead to open society. More institutions and people were included into the knowledge building process became one of the feature of democratic society. As what Hirsh (1987) stated, in democratic society, all citizens need basic knowledge (what Hirsh called cultural literacy) to communicated and involved in democratic interaction. Open to public as part of democratic society, required the public to acknowledge what happened in society, therefore also open learning to all. More literate people with open society may lead to open knowledge condition. Lyotard (1984) claimed that two forms of knowledge: scientific and narrative, and raised the critiques of grand narrative to question hegemony of knowledge and language. In post-modern perspectives, opening up the authorities of knowledge production and respect differences lead knowledge system into more open condition.

In short, the knowledge system in the past was more of close and secret forms. Generally speaking, education only limited to those chosen upper class élite who were able to approach learning and knowledge. These societies formed learning and knowledge as privilege that only open to selected people. Traditionally, the power to declare knowledge was the power to control society thus only restricted to very few. Institutions and social system control over society that made adapting and creating knowledge as exclusive conditions. It was not until the democratic society and post-modernism that knowledge was further open to the public.

Industrial vs. Social Media

Technology improvement of modern age influenced both in industrial and social development. First, the information system changed has made industrial production impact social culture and network uses. According to Masuda (1981), innovational technology changed social economic systems in three stages:

First, in which technology does work previously done by man.

Second, in which technology makes possible work that man has never been able to do before.

Third, in which the existing social and economic structures are transformed into new social and economic systems. (Masuda, 1981, p. 59)

The technology development nowadays, especially on information which mostly referred to media, internet and Web 2.0, changed social and economic structures different from decades ago. Technology influenced production process including knowledge and raise of cyber society.

Technology Influences

As transforming to openness pedagogy, not only the social institutions and system changed, but also technology development played an important role. To begin with, J. Gutenberg started new form of printing books and opened up the potential of sharing knowledge to more people. However, printing itself reduces reproduction cost but does not necessary lead to openness. As Long (2001) claimed, openness of writing and authorship involve social, culture, and economic context. In fact, while education system as described above has been esoteric in many aspects, the technology and art remain open culture for long period of time.

The sharing knowledge can be viewed as part of the culture of technical art development. The ancient technē authors wrote in open form and share to others (Long, 2001). In Greek and Rome, the openness praxis writings were shared only by certain class of readers, especially for governors and military leaders (Long, 2001). By 15th century, open authorship of mechanical arts expanded, while some traditional occult and secrecy topics such as Alchemy, Neoplatonic philosophy, Hermeticism, the cabla, and astral magic also proliferated (Long, 2001).

In 16th century, mining, metallurgy, artillery, and fortification writings represent the open and sometimes collective authorship that practitioners interacted with authors (Long, 2001). The painting, architecture, and arts also communications cross social boundaries that among practitioners and patrons interacted concerning learning, skill, and art works (Long, 2001). In fact, the open and secret perspectives are not separated as clear-cut when come to the technology development.

"These two practice-openness and secrecy-represent, not a contradiction, but separate attitudes concerning dissemination attached to separate kinds of philosophical activities.

Both open and esoteric traditions from the sixteenth century shared, however, an orientation toward manipulating the material world- what might be called a technological or utilitarian orientation" (Long, 2001, p. 248).

The developing of property ideas are related to credit issues. These property concerns change the open concepts from traditional technology and art manufacturing.

Property attitudes toward both inventions and ideas could be used to promote profit and commerce, but they could also be used to gain credit and standing in the courts, the cities, and the universities. Such attitudes first developed among artisans in the context of craft culture, but they were taken up by learned men, particularly those engaged in the new sciences (Long, 2001, p. 249).

The closing of openness in technical manufacturing and concerning property and copyrights seem to be the culture of new science age. This new science age indicates that intellectual copyrights and property are highly respected. However, if knowledge system becomes too restricted and esoteric may limited the knowledge development and innovation. Long (2001) argues that the opening concepts in the past serve the foundation for the science experimental development in 17 century.

I (Long) claim that seventeenth-century struggles to validate new experimental methodologies would not have occurred at all if some of the mechanical arts had not been transformed into discursive disciplines explicated in writing in previous two centuries. An intermediate step occurred: a close associated between technē and praxis. To put it in Aristotelian terms, before technē could join epistemē to become disinterested experimental philosophy, it allied itself with praxis as new political elites of the fifteenth and sixteenth centuries legitimated their power and authority by massive building programs, urban transformations, and conspicuous consumption and also patronized and sometimes themselves engaged in authorship on the mechanical art. During this complex process certain arts were transformed, becoming culturally fit to be used in a philosophical quest concerning nature of the world. (Long, 2001, p. 250)

After this science developing come the Industrious revolution, two main influences changed the education system interests. First, economic structure changed that labor force shifted from farm to industry with develop of welfare system that provided education for citizens. As industrialized producing, agriculture may provide to larger population with less labor working in the field. Other people were shifted to work in the factories or other places. The legal restrict of children labors and some Nations' policy of literacy their people gave most children the opportunity to education. For example, starting from 18 century, Prussia started to required children to attend school and established department for public instruction (Monroe, 1970). In England, Elementary education act was conducted by 1870 that put children education as duty (Meyer, 1972). Public education system was established in modern society and concerned as human rights.

Second, the more complex work in industry required higher human capital. The global completion also increased each nation government to value their human recourse. The starting of knowledge economy and later on creative economy highly emphasized each individual's intellectual ability. Additionally, changes of technology influenced the production process and also knowledge construction. Knowledge construction opened to public through Web 2.0 and social openness development. On one hand, as democratic society encouraged the public to attend public affairs and communications, more people involved social movements and concerned public issues. On the other hand, the technology developments made sharing information and communication easier. Society and technology interaction provided the growing of openness in knowledge production and education. "The theoretical knowledge, the collaborative work style, and the information technologies associated with government-sponsored research and science have indeed become increasingly important elements of society" (Turner, 2006, p. 242).

Technology was not merely mechanic improvement that motivated openness but the influences on cultural and social effects. Heidegger and Foucault both took technology as sense revealing truth and influence human subjectivity (Besley & Peters, 2007). Technology for Heidegger was the united of mind, fine art and human activities to reveal truth (Heidegger, 1977). Foucault followed Heidegger's perspectives of technology as revealing truth and took it further on power relationship and constructing subjectivity (Besley & Peters, 2007). Derrida's inventionalism that indicated the subject openness manner added to human interaction and communication as not mechanic with openness to in-coming others (Bista, 2009). Technology became more biological than mechanistic due to two reasons: first, technologies were more in a sense simultaneous mechanistic and organic; second, when we associated with living organism that technologies were acquiring properties so that self-assembling, self-configuring, self-healing, and cognitive were more resemble living organism (Arthur, 2009). The opening society and technology development encouraged individuals' to express and construct their subjectivities.

Commercial Media and Cyber Society

In modern industrial society, the influences of commercial media and cyber development also promote the development of open pedagogy. The information technology development directly improves the commercial media and cyber working. Since 1950's US department of defense starts the research project, also called Advanced Research Project Agency (ARPA), that connects different computers network, the concept of 'Internet' seems to indicate the new coming era. The commercial use of internet change not only communication forms but also the social interaction. New communication changes social interaction and provides decentralized concepts in identity, nationalism, and citizenship (Tukdeo, 2008).

> The representative technology is no longer a machine with fixed architeculture carrying out a fixed function. It is a system, a network of functionalities—a metabolism of things-executing-things—that can sense its environment and reconfigure its actions to execute appropriately...When a network consists of thousands of separate interacting parts and the environment changes rapidly, it becomes almost impossible to design top-down in any reliable way. Therefore, networks are being designed to "learn" from experience, which simple interactive rules of configuration operate best within different environments (Arthur, 2009:206–207).

The information technology and media developing also influences modern society. Turner (2006) claims that the developing technology is not the only innovation nowadays for those social ideas such as: a disembodied, egalitarian polis, and postinstitutional peer-to-peer market place. In fact, these social ideas can be traced back since 1950's and 1960's developing technology with counterculture movement (Turner, 2006). This counterculture critiques the cold war rational and industrial impact at that time. Some researchers, like Mills (1956), Ellul (1964), Marcuse (1964), Galbraith (1967/1985) and Roszak (1969) provide critical perspectives on the centralized and rationalized society supported by technology development that Turner (2006) states as the counterculture age. In other words, technology and media can be used as industrious ration controlling over individuals. However, technology and media using with critical perspectives can also lead to individual subjective awareness. This freedom of individual occurs the age of personal computer and internet, especially Web 2.0. The new computer technology age that network develops advanced for easy interacting provides opportunities for collective knowledge production. "As computer and computer networks have come on-line, scholars have in turn increasingly shown how these technologies have amplified and accelerated the impact of knowledge and information on production process" (Turner, 2006, p. 242).

The new individuals' relationship is established in this new technology and media era. The peer-to-peer knowledge construction becomes possible again in such cyber society. For learning through information technology or so called long distance learning the relationship among learners, instructors, and technology are based in more open and empowering condition. In learner-learner relationship, instructors need to establish encouraging environment for learners willing to share and help each others (Levin, 2005). Instructors may empower learners by freedom to express and meaningful content for individual learners (Levin, 2005). The proper usage of technology is also important to select technology will be embraced by learners (Levin, 2005). Technology has provided new ways of knowledge production and respects to both teacher (faculty) and students in education institutions as well as in higher education (Gumport & Chun, 2005). In these relationships, the freedom and openness play important role that encourage the interaction and knowledge construction process.

OPEN EDUCATIONAL RESOURCES AND DEMOCRACY

The open resource and interactive culture provides a democratic basis. As the technology improvement that information opens to all individuals, individuals may have the opportunities to interact with social issues and obtain relevant information. Masuda (1981) states the vision of information society can bring true democratic society. In his view, advanced information technology brings individuals to participate social issues. The openness and technology together seem reasonable to expect Masuda's visions. When all citizens have access to knowledge and public issues, the individuals can understand what problems they are dealing with. Therefore, their encounter meaningful social discourses and participate in policy decision making. In addition, while referring to democracy, Dewey has given much attention to democratic education.

An undesirable society, in other words, is one which internally and externally sets up barriers to free intercourse and communication of experience. A society which makes provision for participation in its good for all its member on equal term and which secures flexible readjustment of its institutions through interaction of different forms of associated life is in so far democratic. (Dewey, 1916, p. 99)

The openness knowledge system and education are close to Dewey's perspectives on education and democracy society. In open pedagogy, the open interaction and participation of society can be put into practice into individual level.

Philosophy of Open Pedagogy

The philosophy of OLS pedagogy is constructed of five features, each one making up the various essential aspects of the learning process in the open learning process. The expansion of higher education is pushing pedagogy back on to the agenda: new kinds of students are forcing academics to reconsider how to teach without taking either traditional cultural capital or literacy for granted (O'Shea, 1998). "Students today think and process information differently from their predecessors" (Dale, Holland, and Matthews, 2006, p. 27). They are the first generation to have grown up surrounded by digital technology, whose first port of call for information is, more often than not, Google. Prensky (2001) described these students as "digital natives" and those who have grown up in the pre-digital age as "digital immigrants." The challenge is to provide learning environment that is relevant to digital natives and those who exhibit the characteristics of digital immigrants both of whom work in virtual and real spaces. Their learning space needs to reflect both the curriculum and individual learning styles while providing access to a range of media (Beard and Dale, 2008). In the construction of the OLS pedagogy, we take into account all learners. The pedagogy feature that OLS provides for the scholar/researcher, student, and user is the ability to be open to experiences.

Openness to Experience

The OLS pedagogy provides the opportunity for individuals to take part in their scholarly work though a series of different methods to achieve their outcomes. In OLS, the researcher has the ability to do empirical and inductive research. "Learning is doing and experiencing, but not necessarily conscious: we often act and learn unconsciously, and only a minute part of the experience that forms our learning can be referred to as Knowledge" (Kivinen and Ristelä, 2002, p. 420). In the OLS experiential pedagogy, it is advocated for all to conduct an inquiry-based approach to learning where the use of questions in a prominent role in the teaching process.

OLS experimental pedagogy fosters Francis Bacon's notion of induction. It is our belief that experiential education should be the process by which empirical propositions can be derived from general principles for subsequent testing or questioning. This progression of induction extends human knowledge of the sense world by means of experimentation and empirical observation. Bacon and OLS experiential pedagogy believe that effective knowledge, that is, knowledge as power, arose from the full use of inductive capacities to derive conclusions about the empirical world (Mahootian & Eastman, 2009).

OLS experiential and experimental pedagogy is viewed as individuals conducting experiments that produce constant radical conceptual changes in science that leads to outright abandonment and replacement of old theories and the acknowledgment that empirical research aims of achieving the truth is unreachable. Practical considerations requires science should be linked to the truth in its aim or goal even when it is unachievable. In other words, experimental research should be seen as pursuing the goal of truth if the pursuit of such an unreachable goal can lead to indirect benefits or substantial advantages (Wang-Yen Lee, 2007).

Within this research and learning environment, the OLS pedagogy values a pragmatic form of experiential research and learning. While the scientific approach to creating knowledge is important and valued, it is also critical for the researcher and user to create sets of experiences that translate to individuals who are not affiliated with academia. Users have the ability construct research that is important to the practical everyday world. Knowledge creation within the OLS pedagogy has not hierarchical, but rather what is important for the individual and thus to the community of scholars. By having this approach to research, it alleviates the pressure of having to conform and fosters the freedom of research where peers contribute to the outcomes of the experimental and experiential forms of learning.

Openness to Criticism

An important aspect of OLS pedagogy is the ability for the scholars, teachers, students, and users to be part of critique and self-critical. The practice of self-critiquing and evaluation is essential as a way of helping individuals develop the sense of scholarly voice. It is essential in the OLS pedagogy, that we accept that prior to any experience, we have the deep conviction that reality is, in principle, understandable by us (Procee, 2006). In the open teaching milieu scholars, students, and users posses the ability to deep critical reflection of themselves and their scholarly productions. "Kant believed that the critical task of reason was to single out and to legitimate some *a priori* frameworks in our theoretical and practical knowledge. For Kant's understanding for self critique/reason, the need to presuppose itself, as a datum, which cannot be systematized as an insurmountable critical instance, is a kind of finiteness, not of absoluteness. In the OLS pedagogy, we have adopted the Kantian questions of self critique, "What can I know?," "What ought I to do?," and "What may I hope?" (Pievatolo, 1999, p. 315).

OLS pedagogy also uses the idea of rational deliberation during the process of the self-critique. In the realization that there not everyone will agree on ideas, OLS believes that being open to criticism can be achieved through communication through a rational basis and such communication is a universal condition. "Recognizing the necessity of social interaction for knowledge production, Kant argued in *Critique of Pure Reason (1787)* that human knowledge can be tentatively confirmed or negated only through processes of public submission and critique"(Jackson, 2007, p. 337).

As part of this critiquing process in OLS pedagogy different arguments are proposed and participants justify such arguments as valid by (among other things) using external links to empirical situations. In OLS, critiquing speech is understandable, spoken truthfully and spoken legitimately. OLS places utmost importance on rational debate (participants rely on empirical reasons) over and above other forms of communication. Obviously, it should be noted that by the presence of ranting, personal attacks, and non-listening are signs of non-deliberation and critical reflection (Dunne, 2009).

Openness to Interpretation

An aspect that is essential in OLS is the ability of the teacher and students to be able to have self-expression, free speech, and tied to all of this is academic freedoms, which is the foundation of the university. Academic freedom, often the object of slogans and multifarious activism, is neither a fixed nor an intuitive concept (Salaita, 2008). "Academic autonomy has long been regarded by academics as fundamental for their working lives, as a core value and as 'an essential socio-technical condition of good academic work" (Becher & Kogan, 1992, p. 100). The most important principle of university and scholarly endeavor is the freedom to research and to teach. In the United States, the First Amendment protects artistic and scholarly freedom, as a product of freedom of opinion (Baumanns, 2009).

In the current field of academia, faculty are not necessarily free to take any position they choose, free of judgment about that position. They are subjected to very strenuous kinds of evaluations and judgments about positions that they hold. Therefore, I do not know that academic freedom and freedom of speech are synonymous (Berdahl, et al., 2009). In the OLS environment, we have constructed the policy of freedom that will ensure individuals in the educational environment have the right to express his or herself without the fear of repercussions. Freedom is celebrated and a natural part of the leaning culture. If individuals do not have the ability of self-expression, it seizes to become an open environment of learning. The self-determining freedom of researchers, scholars, and its potential for academic creativity are subject to a wide range of circumstances. Academic freedoms account for these kinds of variations, the national-cultural, and the disciplinary. The self-determining freedom of researchers and scholars is subject to a wide range of conditions, which includes laws, policies, techniques of government and managing, administrative and financial systems, publishing regimes, academic hierarchies, and so on (Marginson, 2008).

The educational milieu in OLS provides educators and students opportunities to share information with one another with the ultimate goal of learning. In doing so, it allows the students to understand the importance of copy written materials along with the key concept of sharing information for the good of the community.

Openness to experience has been singled out as the personality dimension most closely linked to creative behaviors. Individuals with high level of openness to experience are those who are appreciative of novel ideas and new experiences, receptive to a variety of perspectives and thoughts, and unafraid of recruiting unconventional ways to deal with problems at hand; they are also artistic, inventive, and curious (Leung and Chiu, 2008). This aspect of OLS pedagogy perpetuates the necessity for individual expression through scholarship, which is the essential aspect of the OLS process. It is essential in the new paradigm of opening learning and nonhierarchical information sharing that peer reviewed works and the continued form of collaboration continue to exist to better serve the educational community of scholars and students.

Open Science Communication-Technology

Another key feature of OLS pedagogy is the necessity for sharing of information, peer reviewing, trends of cooperation/collaboration with peers and the inclusion of members of the public. Autonomy and academic freedom represent the institutional foundation of each university, but although necessary, are not sufficient to provide modern society with the answers it needs. OLS will contribute to the solution to produce better scholarship.

The competition in research, the pressure from society to transfer scientific knowledge from research to application as quickly as possible, the constant quest for new research funds, and an unstable work situation, confine researchers' activities within strict time schedules does not apply in the OLS pedagogy. It is our view that the OLS pedagogy should produce the knowledge necessary to shape the future by sharing of information and creates space for the long-term development of the diverse forms of knowledge that transcend the need for immediacy. OLS is a place for free and fundamental research (Blasi, 2006).

"Scholarship of teaching and learning has been touted as an instrument of salvation, 'a movement that can transform the nature of ... society toward our ideals of equality and justice. It signals a 'paradigmatic change in higher education" (Atkinson, 2001, p. 1217). Peer review is considered a necessary procedure for assessment of articles, as has traditionally been the case for scholarly journals. Scholarly journals are reliable means of communicating knowledge and findings in a scientific discipline. Researchers rely on articles published in the journals to support and extend their work while acknowledging them in the form of citations (Taneja, Singh, and Raja, 2009).

Most scientific advances are not solely the effect of separate, individual efforts. As the boundaries of scientific disciplines, begin to obscure, the answers to many of today's questions are often are the result of trans-disciplinary approaches to research. Recently there has been increasing interest and investment in trans-disciplinary research teams and centers. By stimulating a wide range of cross-disciplinary collaborations, it allows the facilitation to provide unique opportunities for theory comparison, multiple-behavior research, and the integration of different fields of social and behavioral sciences research.

By eliminating the geographic barriers between research institutions, scientific scholarship has been able to build a professional alliance that values the independent scientific gains made by each individual research project and the joint expertise of our combined resources. Such work promises to provide a stronger basis for advancing our knowledge of the processes by which people maintain health behaviors and how we can best facilitate those processes within and between research institutions, scientific disciplines, and health care providers (Jordan, Ory, and Sher, 2005).

The final aspect is the ability for the public to be involved in the peer reviewing process and collaboration of producing scholarly materials. The OLS environment allows the public user to be involved in the process of contributing to the knowledge community. In this peer-reviewed process outside individuals who are not affiliated with academia provide a perspective that is more pragmatic to the values of the "real world." Often faculty and students only use their disciplines jargon and their research tries to be clever and not necessarily simple and direct in their conclusions.

Openness = Freedom

Another important of OLS pedagogy is the notion of how openness equates to freedom. OLS pedagogy embraces the creative commons understanding it provides scholars, teachers, students, and users the ability of self-expression will benefit the educational community as well as the public. This freedom equates to individuals who use, reuse, and modify information, which serves as the basis for creativity. It is important that information needs to circulate easily in a democratic setting in order to facilitate innovation. If ideas were not easily available to the users of the information, it would slow down the momentum of creating new ideas.

Efficiency requires that information flow be ever freer and cheaper while production incentives simultaneously require information to be costly, partial and deliberately restricted in its availability. From this paradox are born the concepts of intellectual property rights and copyrights – which attempt to reconcile the desire for freedom and free circulation of ideas with the right to control the economic fruits of intellectual work. The OLS provides an interface to allow educators and scholars to distribute and re-use educational materials. Since the earliest days of the internet, copyright issues and intellectual property rights have been among the hottest of hot-button issues for internet users.

Traditionally, intellectual rights management has meant managing the production and distribution of physical copies of a protected work. In a digital environment there are no longer physical copies; instead there is a tendency to regulate intellectual property through technology by incorporating protection mechanisms into digital files, shifting the balance between rights holders and producers on the one hand, and the public, on the other. It is increasingly necessary to come to terms with the implications both of the international system of copyright and patent regulations and of the contradictions within this system.

Education has been commoditized by big business and the legal name of the commodity is copyright (Ronning, 2006).

There are two extremely strong influences regarding copyright protection for online material, an extremely restrictive set of intellectual property laws written before cyberspace existed and on the other, the ubiquity of content that the completely unrestricted and increasingly globalized internet offers to users (Baumman, 2009). This aspect of creative commons is essential in OLS since it provides the opportunity for freedom of scholarship, distribution of scholastic works without fear of repercussions, and thus creates a new form of learning without the constraints of the traditional higher education environment. It places the values of learning from important information, but also that it can be redistributed with the intentions of benefiting the educational system by allowing others to view the desired scholarly works.

A final segment of this creative commons system in OLS is the Openness to Other. That is, most academics write for an informed, albeit limited, circle of scholarly specialists. The communities in the fields of higher education encourage the academic to write for an interested, larger, and wider audience. The *Other* represents individuals outside academia who typically make up the subjects of the scholarship. A key element is that in OLS pedagogy, the *Other* represents a level of respect that academics must give and provide, otherwise, they will continue to have the wall of separation between the scholar and the subject. The *Other* will continue to have the viewpoint that academics continue to live in their "ivory tower."

CONCLUSION

We have outlined the essential aspects of esoteric and open pedagogies containing the key elements that contribute to the OLS form of pedagogy. As demonstrated, the developments of new technologies and open resources within society have fostered the new creation of different forms of pedagogies what we call Open Learning Systems (OLS). The creation and understanding of OLS pedagogy will provide insight into the systematic development of the learning environment. We believe that within the OLS pedagogy scholars, teachers, students, and the public can flourish in all forms of knowledge creation.

Open pedagogy provides a new path for esoteric education that within limited resource combining technology and open ideas, education can be shared with more individuals. Knowledge can be produced can shared with whoever interested in it. Within relevant less resource, more individuals can approach learning and contribute to knowledge creation. In long term, these active interactions may lead to innovations for all studies. While more individuals have the ability to learn and interact in public discourses, education can achieve more equality, and society can become more truly democracy. The field of Education policy should consider open pedagogy as the future form of education and one of many solutions for modern education.

NOTES

[1] That virtue is knowledge, that is, knowledge is a necessary and sufficient condition for virtuous conduct, is an early 'ideology of knowledge'. Socrates tries to establish this on two grounds: since all rational desires are focused on what is good, if one knows what is good, then he or she not act contrary; If one has non-rational desires, but knowledge is sufficient to overcome them, so if one is knowledgeable of goodness, (s)he will not act irrationally.

[2] In this context the interrelations between formalism and modernism need to be investigated but this topic is beyond the scope of this paper.

[3] While we acknowledge Tracy's 'science of the formation of ideas' we want to avoid the political connotations and especially his defense of liberalism. Napoleon in the Institut National first used the term ideology with negative connotations calling Tracy and his colleagues Cabanis, Garat, Wenceslas Jaquemont, Jean-Baptiste Say, François Thurot, among others, 'ideologues' a term later also used derisively by Marx when he called Tracy a *fischblütige Bourgeoisdoktrinär* or 'a fish-blooded bourgeois doctrinaire'.

[4] Plato's Allegory of The Cave explains how can be willfully ignorant of the Forms. They are like prisoners in a cave who can only see the shadows rather than the real objects and who therefore mistake the world of appearances for the world of forms. The analogy must be understood in terms of the larger allegory of the cave, the sun and the divided line. Plato's famous allegory establishes the importance of understanding and interpreting symbolism and the need to embrace a hermeneutics that gets us beyond the mere order of words or literal understanding or translation.

[5] For this early Christian literature see http://www.earlychristianwritings.com/gnostics.html.

[6] See http://www.nationalgeographic.com/lostgospel/?fs=www9.nationalgeographic.com and see http://www.earlychristianwritings.com/gospeljudas.html for translation of the gospel. The story behind the recovery of the gospel is quite staggering. It was offered on to the art market in 1983 for $3 million and then sat in a New York bank vault until 1989; bought in 1999 by a Swiss dealer Frieda Nussberger-Tchacos who entrusted them to US dealer/philanthopist Bruce Ferrini who broke them up and sold them individually. One codex-the Gospel of Judas-was eventually sold to the US National Geographical Society which published them. I base this account on Roger Pearse's web page at http://www.tertullian.org/rpearse/manuscripts/gospel_of_judas/.

[7] See The Catholic Encyclopedia on secret societies at http://www.newadvent.org/cathen/14071b.htm.

REFERENCES

Arthur, W.B. (2009). *The Nature of Technology*. New York, NY: Free Press.

Atkinson, M.P. (2001). "The Scholarship of Teaching and Learning: Reconceptualizing Scholarship and Transforming the Academy". *Social Forces, 79*(4), 1217–1230.

Baumann, M. (2009). "An Insider's Guide to Creative Commons". *Information Today, 26*(9), 15.

Baumanns, H. (2009). "The Future of Universities and the Fate of Free Inquiry and Academic Freedom". *Social Research, 76*(3), 795–804.

Beard, J. & Dale, P. (2008). "Redesigning Services for the Net-gen and Beyond: A Holistic Review of Pedagogy, Resource, and Learning Space". *New Review of Academic Librarianship, 14*, 99–114.

Becher, T. & Kogan, M. (1992). *Process and Structure In Higher Education* (2nd ed.). London: Routledge.

Berdahl, R. M., Gray, H. H., Kerrey, B., Marx, A., Vest, C. M. & Westphal, J. (2009). "Free Inquiry and Academic Freedom: A Panel Discussion Among Academic Leaders". *Social Research, 76*(2), 731–766.

Besley, A.C. & Peters, M.A. (2007). *Subjectivity and Truth: Foucault, Education, and the Culture of Self*. New York: Peter Lang.

Biesta, G. (2009). "Education after Deconstruction: Between Event and Invention," in M. Peters & G. Biesta (Eds.), *Derrida, Deconstruction, and the Politics of Pedagogy*. New York: Peter Lang, 97–114.

Blasi, P. (2006). "The European University – Towards a Wisdom-based Society," *Higher Education in Europe 31*(4): 403–407.

Breton (1934). *What is Surrealism*. Retrieved from: http://www.generation-online.org/c/fcsurrealism2.htm

Breton, A, (1924). *Manifesto of Surrealism*. Retrieved from: http://www.poetryintranslation.com/PITBR/French/Manifesto.htm

Compayré, G. (1900). *The History of Pedagogy*. London: Swan Sonnenschein.

Cubberley, E. (1920). *The History of Education: Educational Practice and Progress Considered as a Phase of the Development and Spread of Western Civilization*. Boston, MA: Houghton Mifflin.

Dale, P., Holland, M. & Matthews, M., (Eds.) (2006). *Subject Librarians: Engaging* with the Learning and Teaching Environment. Guildford: Ashgate.

Dewey, J. (1916). *Democracy and Education: An Introduction to the Philosophy of Education*. New York: The free press.

Dunne, K. (2009). "Cross Cutting Discussion: A Form of Online Discussion Discovered within Local Political Online Forums," *Information Polity: The International Journal of Government & Democracy in the Information Age, 14*(3), 219–232.

Galbraith, J.K. (1967/1985). *The New Industrial State*. 4th ed. Boston: Houghton Mifflin.

Gumport, P.J. & Chun, M. (2005). "Technology and Higher Education: Opportunities and Challenges for the New Era," in P.G. Altbach, R.O. Berdahl, & P.J. Gumport (Eds.) (2005). *American Higher Education in the Twenty-first Century: Social, Political, and Economic Challenges,* 2nd Edition, pp. 393–424. Baltimore, Maryland: The John Hopkins University press.

Heidegger, M. (1977). *The Question Concerning Technology and Other Essays*, W. Lovitt (trans.). New York, NY: Garland.

Hirsch, E.D. (1987). *Cultural Literacy, What Every American Needs to Know*. Boston, MA: Houghton Mifflin.

Jordan, P.J., Ory, M.G. & Sher, T.G. (2005). "Yours, Mine, and Ours: The Importance of Scientific Collaboration in Advancing the Field of Behavior Change Research," *Annals of Behavioral Medicine* 29: 7–10.

Kant, I. (1787). *Critique of Pure Reason*. Retrieved from: http://www.rlwclarke.net/courses/LITS3303/2011-2012/01Kant,CritiqueofPureReason.pdf

Kivinen, O. & Ristelä, P. (2002). "Even Higher Learning Takes Place by Doing: from Postmodern Critique to Pragmatic Action," *Studies in Higher Education 27*(4): 419–430.

Lee, W.Y. (2007). "A Pragmatic Case against Pragmatic Scientific Realism," *Journal for General Philosophy of Science, 38*(2): 299–313.

Leung, A. K.-Y. & Chiu, C. (2008). "Interactive Effects of Multicultural Experiences and Openness to Experiences on Creative Potential," *Creativity Research Journal 20*(4): 376–382.

Levin, S.J. (2005). "Creating a Foundation for Learning Relationships," in S.J. Levin (Ed.), *Making Distance Education Work: Understanding Learning and Learners at a Distance*. Okemos, MI: LearnerAssociates.net LLC, 17–24.

Long, P.O. (2001). *Openness, Secrecy, Authorship: Technical Arts and the Culture of Knowledge from Antiquity to the Renaissance*. Baltimore, MD: John Hopkins University Press.

Lyotard J.F. (1984). *The Postmodern Condition: A Report on Knowledge*. G. Bennington and B. Massumi(Trans.). MN, Manchester: University of Manchester Press.

Mahootian, F. & Eastman, T.E. (2009). "Complementary Frameworks of Scientific Inquiry: Hypothetico-deductive, Hypothetico-inductive, and Observationalinductive," *World Futures: The Journal of General Evolution 65*(1): 61–75.

Marcuse, H. (1964). *One-dimensional Man: Studies in Ideology of Advanced Industrial Society*. Boston, MA: Beacon.

Marginson, S. (2008). "Academic Creativity under New Public Management: Foundations for an Investigation," *Educational Theory 58*(3): 269–287.

Marx, K. & Engels, F. (1970). *The German Ideology*, C.J. Arthur (Ed.). New York, 46–47.

Masuda, Y. (1981). *The Information Society as Post-industrial Society*. Bethesda, MD: World Future Society.

Meyer, J.W. (1972). *Theories of the Effects of Education on Civic Participation in Developing Societies*. New York: Asia Society.

Mills, C.W. (1956). *The Power Elite*. New York: Oxford University Press.

Monroe, P. (1970). *A Text-book in the History of Education*. New York: AMS Press.

O'Shea, A. (1998). "A Special Relationship? Cultural Studies, Academia and Pedagogy," *Cultural Studies, 12*(4): 513–527.

Pievatolo, M.C. (1999). "The Tribunal of Reason: Kant and the Juridical Nature of Pure Reason," *Ratio Juris, 12*(3): 311–327.

Prensky, M. (2001). "Digital Natives, Digital Immigrants," *On the Horizon, 9*(5): 1–6.

Procee, H., (2006). Reflection in education: A Kantian Epistemology. Retrieved from: http://cms.kcn. unima.mw:8002/moodle/downloads/chilemba/My%20Documents/PhD%20articles/kant%20and%20 reflection.pdf

Ronning, H. (2006). "Systems of Control and Regulation: Copyright Issues, Digital Divides and Citizens' Rights," *Critical Arts: A South-North Journal of Cultural & Media Studies, 20*(1): 20–34.

Roszak, T. (1969). *The Making of a Counter Culture: Reflections on the Technocratic Society and Its Youthful Opposition*. Garden City, NY: Doubleday.

Salaita, S. (2008). "Curricular Activism and Academic Freedom: Representations of Arabs and Muslims in Print and Internet Media," *Arab Studies Quarterly, 30*(1): 1–14.

Stanley, T. (1701). *History of Philosophy*. Berkeley, CA: Apocryphile Press.

Taneja, A., Singh, A. & Raja M.K. (2009). "Journals and Their Emerging Roles in Knowledge Exchange," *Communications of the ACM, 52*(11): 125–131.

Tukdeo, S. (2008). The power of P2P: Information networks, social organizing and education futures. In M. A. Peters & R. G. Britez. (Eds.) (2008). *Open education and education for openness*, pp. 43–55. Rotterdam, the Netherlands: Sense.

Turner, F. (2006). *From Counterculture to Cyberculture: Steward, the Whole Earth Network, and the Rise of Digital Utopianism*. Chicago, IL: The University of Chicago Press.

Wang-Yen L. (2007). A pragmatic case against pragmatic scientific realism. *Journal for General Philosophy of Science, 38*(2), 299–313.

CHAPTER 4

OPEN LEARNING SYSTEMS: THE NEXT EVOLUTION OF EDUCATION

INTRODUCTION

Education has come in many forms and is always seeking the next *magic bullet* to solve the problems of the masses in hopes of establishing credibility among the other disciplines. Now we are not stating that we have created the ultimate resolution to solve the world's educational problem. What we have done is constructed a new paradigm in which education can be constructed and has the ability to better educate those who are have the desire in the creative economies. The establishment of the Open Learning System (OLS) provides student, learners, educators, and administrators the ability to take a step back from the (educational structures) forest that it has become and view the educational tree (OLS) through the lens of the creative economy. As we will demonstrate there is an ever-growing momentum shift of world economies and the absolute necessity for educational institutions and nations to begin to change their thought processes in terms of education, otherwise there will be a lagging ability to adapt to the more progressive forms form of education (OLS). In this article, we will provide the origins of OLS, current problems of educational pedagogy, and innovations of OLS to the educational processes.

Several ideas have emerged with the concept of Open Learning. First, *Open Epistemology,* which primarily reduces the restriction of prior knowledge. The Second, *Constructivism,* is the ability for individuals to construct social meanings. Third, *Connectionism,* examines how the mind works. Fourth, *Social Criticism,* the awareness of individual identity and subjectivity expression is important to reflect ideology and put into practice in daily living. Fifth, *Post-Modernism Movement,* concepts which critique the grand narratives and value individual, minor expressions, and meanings. Finally, the Sixth, *Technology Development,* this is the transformation of information into digital forms and becomes knowledge.

ORIGINS OF THE CONCEPT & PRECURSOR

Open Epistemology

Known knowledge and theories is the base to explore further unknown phenomena. However, from human history, some knowledge authority restricted the development of new knowledge. The knowledge and power relationship will be further discussed in *Post-Modern Movement* section and what the focus here is the epistemology development. Popper (1963) stated the falsified theory that new knowledge replaces old one in term of phenomena falsified prior knowledge or theory. This perspective leads the process of evolution in epistemology. Kuhn (1962) also claimed the scientific paradigm changes influenced how science investigates data and determines truth. The knowledge truthiness relays on which paradigm and methodology approaches instead of just adapting one determine perspective. The justifications multiple knowledge forms are supporting the assumptions is that openness of epistemology becomes important. Openness embraces new perspectives and methods toward knowledge development. Open learning contains attitudes of open epistemology which encourages continual development of knowledge for future societal changes.

Constructivism

An individual's approach to society along with interacting with others will construct new meanings. This perspective leads to the idea of open meanings and the construction of new individual meanings. Individuals take an active role in constructing new meanings from what they have observed in their environment or society. This is different from being a passive observer and learner, which accepts the given objective environment. Piaget (1932) pointed out that meanings were constructed based on individual development and interaction with peers. Von Glasersfeld (1995) stated 'radical constructivism' that emphasized the important of subjective constructing meanings to adapt social living instead of finding external reality.

Social constructivism implies the importance of social influence. In education, these ideas lead to the respect of individuals learning and constructing meanings of their own, as well as improving cooperative process that through interaction among teachers and students may lead to broader experience and meaningful constructing knowledge. In open learning systems, all members in the system have the authority to construct their own meanings over learning materials. OLS provides an interacting environment and cooperation opportunities that help members to combine different experiences and extend their experiences for constructing meaning.

Connectionism

The connectionism, which mainly concerns neural networks, views knowledge learning as units networking process. In addition, connectionism provides how the mind works in brain. The human brain is a neural network that contains the connections among neurons units and connections (synapses) to operate. The connectionism of neurons networking may provide how humans conduct cognition. Some researches based on connectionism provide how human operate their brains and try to generalize learning methods, such as Hinton(1992), Sejnowski and Rosenberg(1987), Rumelhart and McClelland (1986) etc. The input units (learning) toward output units (react) involve the hidden units of process of mind operation. The connection weights become important part of establishing learning model in connectionism. In open learning systems, knowledge learning is based on individual difference and provides various learning models to fit individual needs. The form of input knowledge in OLS provides diverse forms for individuals to learn and make easier connections in their neurons networks.

Social Criticism

Social criticism provides an opportunity for reflection and self-expression. Adorno (1966) critiqued cultural industrious that transform individuals into one dimension people. Individuals lost reflection ability and negative dialection opportunity. Habermas (1984) also claimed the importance of communication action and social interaction. The social power may influence rational communication in real world and Habermas declared fulfilling the four elements of discourse: comprehensibility, truth, rightness, and truthfulness as the rational discourse that releases subjectivity from social technology and the rationing of power control. Educational systems should provide individuals the opportunity to analyze social ideology and inter-subjective communication. OLS provides an environment that promotes open interaction and open communication. Individuals will gain the opportunity for reflection on different issues with critical perspectives that will lead to social critical perspectives. The encouraging and respecting of openness interaction also provides opportunities for inter-subjective communication.

Post-Modernism Movement

The post-modernism questioned grand narrative and respected for hierological difference among individuals. Lyotard (1979/1984) pointed out grand narratives could not fulfill society multiple dimensions. Baudrillard (1998) critiqued commercialize society that individuals were controlled by media and lack of social concerns lead to 'the death of society'. Rorty further critiqued traditional foundation philosophy. On one hand Rorty (1979) brought out 'anti-essentialism' that rejected 'objective truth' that consider the possibility of different changing truthiness.

On the other hand, he stated 'anti-representationalism' that knowledge was not simply internal mind reflecting of external world. Additionally, Rorty (1989) further critique western 'logos-centrism' and led to 'new-pragmatism' that justified the value of multiple knowledge system. The self-creation to relief from 'final vocabulary' that contingency is partially ignore others to open up to self own creation (Rorty, 1989). Post-modernism movement gave the chance of decentralized and respecting differences that all individuals have the rights and authority of their own expressions. OLS combines different resources and respects a different perspective that contributes to the decentralization of ideas that grand narratives no longer dominate knowledge system. Different individual theories and fields of knowledge could be preserved and shared in OLS. Multiple knowledge and values are respected in OLS and lead to the creative and cooperative knowledge system. Members are encouraged to express their unique ideas and in cooperation with others to produce new knowledge.

Technology Development

The next concept that contributes to Open Learning Systems is the developing of technology, especially the internet interaction and digitalization of the written text. Since 2000, technology development has become more user-friendly for personal use along with the improving access of information. The increasing access and interaction through internet has brought the opportunity for distance learning and open learning environments.

OLS uses technology development as the innovation to transform knowledge from traditional (hard copy) text into a digital form that reduces the cost for whoever is interested. This is significant because instead of buying the traditional books and finding places for storage, individuals now can easily purchase information, store it, and more importantly, shared it. In addition, OLS provides cooperative knowledge building environments that all members of OLS can share their thoughts and create new knowledge through interacting with different perspectives. The new Web 2.0 and user friendly developing of technology gave OLS the chance to make user easily approach and take advantage to increase learning capital. This presumes that open education is knowledge based on social construction and conducting community networks may help knowledge building (Cambridge, 2008).

The changes provide broader knowledge resources access and new education ecology from traditional education environments (Iiyoshi & Kumar, 2008). These origins lead to the foundation for developing OLS that respects individual ideas and creates an environment for individual expression, interaction and cooperative creativity. OLS provides the ability for open education issues, which is concerned with open resource and open access.

Part 2: Open Education & Openness

Part 3: The Changing Theoretical Context: The Creative Economy

Although knowledge and its distribution has been the key driver of economic development, today knowledge-based firms gain competitive advantages through their ability to use, process, analyze and share powerful information and communication technologies at an unprecedented scale and speed. In order to establish an economy that relies primarily on the use of ideas rather than on physical abilities, and on the application of technology rather than on the transformation of raw materials, neoliberals have promoted a formidable re-engineering process of the previously established productive paradigm. In order to meet the needs of the post-Fordist accumulation regime, organizational changes such as forms of subcontracting and or outsourcing, "just-in-time" production and the like have been introduced (Orsi, 2009).

The important point is that the knowledge and creative economies are not just created from ideology. This process demonstrates the need for scholars to describe, analyze, and explained the occurrences that are being constructed (Peters, 2009). It is because of this dramatic shift in forming creative economies that higher education is destined to change and become part of the central focus in the creative economy and the OLS curriculum structure serves as the next level of what it means to educate in the creative economy. Creative economy values the knowledge and potential of creativity to extend the economic profit. The transforming knowledge with creativity may become the new form of production and require high human capital. From knowledge economy toward recent creative economy, the relationship among knowledge, learning, network and economy has more interaction and complexity. Some researches and studies have concluded the creativity within knowledge economy society is the new economical innovation, such as Florida (2002), Grabher (2001), Howkins (2000), O'connor (1999), Power and Scott (2004), Pratt (1997), and Scott (2000).

The creative economy era value the production of knowledge capitalism; therefore concerns strong connection between education system and knowledge efficiency. For example, this shift ideology brings the changes for the higher education since the 1980's and researches show that neo-liberalism plays an important role and consider economical contribution. The neo-liberalism arises and transforms of 'new public management' influence the higher education institutions and change the justification of their existence (Olssen & Peters, 2005).

"The traditional professional culture of open intellectual enquiry and debate has been replaced with a institutional stress on performativity, as evidenced by the emergence of an emphasis on measured outputs: on strategic planning, performance indicators, quality assurance measures and academic audits" (Olssen & Peters, 2005, 313).

The combine ideology of knowledge economy and education make human resource idea into education system and call for human capital. Knowledge production is no longer from limited authority people, but open to the public and individuals to contribute knowledge producing and creating.

OLS provides the knowledge cooperative and creative production. The openness provides the basic elements of creativity that all ideas are encouraged and shared. In addition, In creative economy, nationwide concerns how to improve human capital and transform creativity into practical economic production. Interacting learning opportunity in OLS also gives the environment of cooperative creating knowledge and seeking ways of transforming into economy practice.

Part 4: Open Learning Systems and the Problem of the Curriculum

Educational curriculums have been written about in many forms and structures. For an open learning system to be effective, it must be a fluid form, which allows individuals to benefit from the many forms of open learning environment. This system provides a foundation approach towards establishing a productive form of shared systems. Creative thinking is often the product of collective knowledge, the result of individuals sharing ideas and knowledge freely in order to achieve the best possible results. Knowledge that is collectively shared continues to grow and change because of continuous questioning and improvement through the combined efforts of its contributors (Nelson, Christopher, & Mims, 2009). It is because of this understanding that the OLS curriculum design incorporates many ideas from traditional systems theory and the theoretical perspective of open learning. The purpose is a conduit to permit open sharing of information and knowledge transferring creators to the learners.

Excess of Information & Content

In the Open Learning System, the design structure is a filter of knowledge and information. It has the ability to take all forms of information and provide a structure for a filter of information. The increased interest in knowledge discovery, knowledge management, and knowledge transfer can be attributed to many factors including the advances in information and communication technologies; data explosion and information overload and, the need for organizations to better utilize their intellectual capital.

This swift pace of growth in digitized information makes it imperative for OLS to seek alternative methods to effectively and efficiently utilize these invaluable assets. In order to assist the learner/user with the problem of information overload and not exacerbate it, these new methods should go beyond what is already available to the knowledge worker today.

"Over the last twenty years, the Internet has transformed the way in which information is created, stored, and accessed. We are now all experiencing a "data deluge" on a global scale. The "needles" of information that we require may be the same size as before; but the "haystack" in which they are contained has grown infinitely larger and will continue to grow" (Baker, 2008, p. 1).

The OLS structure does this by serving as a warehouse of information with the preconception that the information provided and used in OLS is a peer-to-peer evaluation system. As a collective, OLS serves to determine which information is more valid and reliable. In this capacity, users will have access to whatever necessary information that is desired, but there may be some limitations and critical evaluations of the information to ensure the quality and academic integrity of the information used.

Validation of Information & Standards

With the advent of *Wikipedia* and other open sources of information, it has spurned the notion of the validity of the information produced and to the recognition of the sources used in creating to information. In the academic tradition, information is through books and journals, not through websites and multimedia productions. "The fact that a system which is fit for one purpose will not necessarily be fit for all purposes is a fundamental consideration when evaluating the legitimacy of proposals. It is one of the most important messages for policy-makers to understand" (Newton, 2007, 149).

It takes a mind shift in the approach of validating new scholarship. *Wikipedia* has become a resource for scholars and students for starting a new research endeavor. Within the OLS concept, the ability to use the *Wikipedia's* of the world, rather than digging first thing into the typical libraries has validated the concept of useful knowledge. Within higher education, faculty have and are beginning to acknowledge the practicality and usefulness of online information, but most are still not ready to consider it a valid source of information worthy of academic scholarship. In the OLS design, shared information and knowledge production are at the same level of peer review and critique can still be applicable. The modern researcher can utilize the digital media as a starting point to.

Diversity of New Media

"Virtual reality is "immersive," which means that it is a technology of mediation whose purpose is to disappear. Yet this disappearing act is made difficult by the apparatus that virtual reality requires" (Bolter and Grusin, 1996). The variety in the forms of informational new media is problematic. Technology has transformed that notion of the print media and the inclusion of digital photographs, websites and online videos. Jay Bolter and Richard Grusin argue in *Remediation (1996)* that there is a slight paradox in digital media, in which the development of digital media has focused on increasing both immediacy and hypermediacy. They continue to state that digital media has become aggressive in its remediation of older forms of media.

The new technology created and developed is creating problems for the users to be able to learn in different ways than every predicted. In OLS, there is an embracing philosophy of technology in the learning process.

"Multimedia has the potential to create high quality learning environments. The key elements of multiple media, user control over the delivery of information, and interactivity can be used to enhance the learning process through creating integrated learning environments. Explanation can be combined with illustrative examples, online assessment with feedback and the user can be provided with opportunities to practice and experiment. A range of media elements can be used to convey a given message and the user can study at a time and place convenient to them, taking as long or as little as they need" (Cairncross & Mannion, 2001, 156).

The structure in OLS provides the environment for the curriculum to adopt emerging technologies will be implemented with advanced and sound instruction to promote interactive learning by engaging learners in actively analyzing information and knowledge construction and applying technology to support their decision-making (Chih-Hsiung, 2005). In this enriched multimedia environment that currently exists, the topic of (online) collaboration may appear only marginally relevant to academics, but with cell phones, e-mail, multiplayer online games, mailing lists, Weblogs and wikis, our everyday lives are increasingly enmeshed with technology. Acknowledging that access to technology is partial and generally limited to people in societies that benefit from the globalization of the information.

It is urgent that we examine as scholars and educators the ways in which we collaborate through technological channels.

Development of User-Content

The traditional form of education systems is hierarchical in nature and that all information and knowledge is transferred and created by the State curriculum and the respective teachers. In OLS, the development of user-content by teachers and students in the co-production of knowledge shatters the old ways of knowledge production. In the structure of OLS, the shared responsibility of learning and knowledge production is on a continual basis. By tapping into Howard Gardner's multiple intelligences, it allows both the teacher and student to be shared informers and recipients of information. The OLS is a group of very versatile web applications, which provide easy interaction between users. They can edit articles, share files and communicate with other users.

> For a learning system to be interactive for different types of learner, it will be necessary to take account of the users (the learners) who are expected to use such systems for learning, and it is not merely enough to give students access to different tools and/or learning environments (Bates & Leary, 2001).

It requires a move from a teacher–student dependence design to a teacher–student independence design that gives students flexibility and control over their learning in line with their changing needs. This essentially requires investigation of factors such as learners' different learning preferences, needs, interests, prior knowledge, experiences, background, culture, talents and abilities (Sabry and Barker, 2009).

In the last few years, these applications demonstrated a big potential in allowing users to actively participate in publishing content on the web. User-generated content quickly grew into the largest source of information on the web. This quick development was not really expected or predicted, it was a matter of some innovative experiments. With improvements in technology, making the servers able to store large capacities of data and developing applications, which are in the first place simple to use, one thing led to another, and web turned into a platform for cooperation (Snuderl, 2008).

Most of these web applications share the same basic principles. They allow users to edit articles (different Wiki systems) or share files (videos, photos, presentations, documents). Anonymous access usually allows users only to view uploaded information or files, but users who register and log in can also comment, rate, bookmark and upload their own content. Exposing all content to other users makes users follow self-censorship principles – this and different moderation models (quality controls by moderators) lead to constant improvements of the overall quality. Letting the users organize the content of the website in a new and interactive way is an opportunity to overcome problems originating from strict category classification of items and different terminologies. Higher engagement of experienced users could help us learn about our users better and finally yet importantly, following a common approach when defining the ontology model English tags could also be shared on international level (Snuderl, 2008).

Traditional Textbook

In many people's experience, the first serious engagement with books, reading, and knowledge happens when they encounter textbooks in school. Yet schoolbooks tend to be forgotten by their readers, and consequently neglected by scholarship, pushed deep into personal and collective memory and supplanted by the genres, disciplines and formats that adults know. The schoolbook is not only unglamorous, its theory is subtle and its methodology complex (Leslie Howsam et al., 2007). Some would argue that in the era of digital media, the traditional textbook is dead. It has become an arcane idea of informational knowledge, which fits the industrial age of mass education.

"Instructional principles and practice have moved away from an emphasis on learning as reproducing knowledge to learning as transforming knowledge, from rote learning to meaningful learning. The needs to improve the quality of learning and advocated a more learner-centered approach in which the various needs and circumstances of learners are recognized" (Cairncross & Mannion, 2001, 156).

However, the traditional paper textbooks are the backbone for instruction, but electronic "hypertext" is increasingly common. Libraries often distribute reserve readings online instead of circulating paper copies, generally in portable document file format (PDF). In addition, universities are heavily investing in course-management learning systems such as WebCT and Blackboard. These systems often provide and integrate online readings directly into the course. This can be done through links to external Web sites or document files stored on the school's servers The bookstore may not be able to get a paper copy to students in time, but electronic copies can be made available quickly and cheaply. This approach can make readings accessible when a student lives in another state or country (Vernon, 2006).

In this ever-growing series of issues of technology taking hold in the educational arena, students have evolved as learners. The traditional forms of learning have changed into a dynamic process of interactive learning. In the OLS structure, students have the ability to use all forms of information that provide the best forms of understanding. The OLS has the ability to adapt and tap into providing the information needed to enhance various learning experiences.

CONCLUSION

It is apparent from the ideas presented that OLS is a new way of viewing curriculum and education systems. OLS has the ability to be adopted by the multiversity that currently envelopes our current university systems and demonstrates the ability to appeal to a mass audience of learners, not just those housed at universities and colleges. We provided the origins of OLS, current problems of educational pedagogy, and innovations of OLS to the educational processes. The establishment of the Open Learning System provides educators and administrators the ability to take a step back and view the educational process through the lens of the creative economy. There is an ever-growing momentum shift by institutions of higher education, nations, and world economies to begin to change their thought processes in terms of education, otherwise there will be a lagging ability to adapt to the more progressive forms form of education Open Learning Systems.

REFERENCES

Adorno, T.W. (1966). *Negative Dialectics*, Translated by E.B. Ashton (1973). London: Routledge.

Bates, B. & Leary, J. (2001). Supporting a range of learning styles using a taxonomy-based design framework approach. *Proceedings of the Annual Conference of Australian Society for Computers in Learning and Tertiary Education*. Retrieved from http://www.ascilite.org.au/conferences/melbourne01/pdf/papers/batesb.pdf

Baudrillard, J. (1998). *The consumer society: myths and structures*. London ; Thousand Oaks, Calif.: Sage.

Bolter, J.D. & Grusin, R. (1996). Remediation. The Johns Hopkins University Press.

Cairncross, S. & Mannion, M. (2001). Interactive Multimedia and Learning: Realizing the Benefits. *Innovations in Education and Teaching International*. Taylor & Francis Ltd.

Cambridge, B. (2008). Scaffolding for systemic change. In T. Iiyoshi & V. Kumar (Eds.) (2008). *Opening up education*, 357–374, Cambridge, Massachusetts: The MIT press.

Chih-Hsiung. T. (2005). From presentation to interaction: new goals for online learning technologies. *Educational Media International, 42*(3), 189–206.

Florida R. (2002). *The rise of the creative class*. New York: Basic Books.

Glasersfeld, E. von (1995). *Radical constructivism: A way of knowing and learning*. London: Falmer Press.

Grabher G, (2001). "Ecologies of creativity: the Village, the Group, and the heterarchic organisation of the British advertising industry" *Environment and Planning A, 33*(2): 351–374.

Hinton, G., "How Neural Networks Learn from Experience, *Scientific American* (September, 1992): 145–151.

Howkins, J. (2001). *The Creative Economy: How people make money from ideas*, London: Penguin.

Iiyoshi, T. & Kumar, V. (2008). *Conclusion: New pathways for shaping the collective Agenda to open up education*. In T. Iiyoshi & V. Kumar (Eds.) (2008). *Opening up education*, 429–440, Cambridge, Massachusetts: The MIT press.

Kuhn, T. S. (1962). *The Structure of Scientific Revolutions*. Chicago: University of Chicago press.

Leslie Howsam, L., Stray, C., Jenkins, A., Secord, J.A. & Vaninskaya, A. What the victorians learned: Perspectives on nineteenth-century schoolbooks.

Lyotard, J.F. (1979/1984). *The postmodern condition: a report on knowledge*. Translated by G. Bennington & B. Massumi. Minneapolis: University of Minnesota Press.

O'CONNOR, J. (1999). *The Definition of 'Cultural Industries'* Retrieved from: http:// www.mipc.mmu.ac.uk/iciss/reports/defin.pdf

Olssen, M. & Peters, M. A. (2005). Neoliberalism, higher eduction and the knowledge economy: From the free market to knowledge capitalism. *Journal of Education Policy, 20*(3), 313–345.

Orsi, Cosma. (2009). Knowledge-based society, peer production and the common good. *Capital & Class Academic One File*.

Paul E. Newton, P.E. (2007). Clarifying the purposes of educational assessment. *Assessment in Education. 14*(2), 149–170.

Peters, M., Marginson, S, & Murphy, P. (2009). Creativity and the global knowledge economy. New York: Peter Lang.

Peters, M.A. (2009). Education, creativity, and the economy of passion. In M.A. Peters, S. Marginson, and P. Murphy (Eds.). *Creativity, and the global knowledge economy,* pp. 125–148. London and New York: Peter Lang.

Piaget, J. (1932). *The Moral Judgment of the Child.* London: Kegan Paul, Trench, Trubner and Co.

Popper, K. (1963). *Conjectures and Refutations,* London: Routledge and Keagan Paul.

Pratt, A., (1997). The Cultural Industries Sector: Its definition and character from secondary sources on Employment and trade, Britain 1984–1991, London: *London School of Economics Department of Geography and Environment, Research papers in Environment and spatial analysis, no. 41.*

Rorty, R. (1979). *Philosophy and the Mirror of Nature.* Princeton: Princeton University Press.

Rorty, R. (1989). *Contingency, Irony, and Solidarity.* Cambridge: Cambridge University Press.

Rumelhart, D. & McClelland, J. (1986). On Learning the Past Tenses of English Verbs. In J. McClelland & D. Rumelhart et al. *Parallel Distributed Processing: Explorations in the Microstructure of Cognition,* 216–271, Cambridge, Mass.: The MIT press.

Sabrya, K. & Barkerb, J. (2009). Dynamic Interactive Learning Systems. *Innovations in Education and Teaching International. 46*(2), 185–197.

Scott, A. J. & Power, D. (2004). *Cultural Industries and the Production of Culture.* London: Routledge.

Snuderl, K. (2008). Tagging: Can user-generated content improve our services? Statistical *Journal of the IAOS,* 125–132.

Scott A. J. (2000). *The cultural economy of cities.* London: Sage.

Sejnowski, T. & Rosenberg, C. (1987). Parallel networks that Learn to Pronounce English Text, *Complex Systems,* 1 (1987): 145–168.

CHAPTER 5

THE ECONOMICS OF OPEN EDUCATION

INTRODUCTION

Institutions of higher education are facing problems in meeting employment, utilizing new technology while staying globally competitive for faculty and research. I believe that educational leaders, teachers, and policy makers have to respond to the provision of individualized mass education with a greater sense of quality assurance and at a lower financial cost. The university's role in the nation's economy is to increase its ability to transfer research to industry, generate new inventions and patents. There has been a movement in the U.S. and around the world to make universities the centers of innovation. The idea of open learning innovation in the peer to peer system of higher education has been put into the forefront of economic, social, and cultural creative concepts. Open learning and open innovation provide educators and administrators in the peer-to-peer networks the ability view the educational process through the lens of the creative economy. In doing so, there is push to embrace open innovation and the necessity to use peer-to-peer networks by educational institutions.

Society and industry are increasingly becoming more dependent on innovation in the science and entertainment. Shared knowledge evolves and is always changing because of the continuous questioning by the participants and the knowledge is improved through the combined efforts of its contributors (Nelson, Christopher, & Mims, 2009). One of the many roles of institutions is to increase its ability to transfer research to industry, generate new inventions, patents, and spin-off its technology. As such, there has been a movement in the U.S. and around the world to make universities centers of innovation, and to enhance their ability to commercialize their research.

Openness and peer-to-peer (P2P) networks are driving forces to knowledge creation and social and economic advancement through the development of a knowledge society. Openness and P2P are increasingly receiving high degrees of attention from scholars, professionals, and policy makers in recent years. A growing number of publications and conferences are exploring the subjects from various angles. Openness and P2P are becoming essential ideas in the growing area of policy development in higher education. Technology frequently changes a culture's norms and requires societies to stay current in the evolving culture. Some faculty and administrators believe by simply providing reasonable hi-tech infrastructures is all that is required to develop and maintain effective technological pedagogy. It is essential for educational systems to provide opportunities for students to develop practical and cognitive skills (Langer & Knefelkamp, 2008).

Since open education is a new paradigm, many faculty members are unprepared for the fundamental differences in the roles required for teaching online. A higher level of involvement by administrators in faculty support is needed to ensure success. As higher education faces competition for nontraditional adult students, it is important for faculty and administration to identify the needs of their adult students. Institutions must understand student's preferences in using online learning and ensure they take those preferences to heart when planning their e-learning courses and degree programs. It is no surprise that adult students have different learning needs and expectations, which of course sets them apart from their traditional students. The extensive body of literature has established clear emphasis for adult educators and that adult learning has become an important factor in American education (Ausburn, 2004).

The rising speed of economic change in new technologies and the presumed increase in the rate of depreciation of knowledge and skills have forced the move toward lifelong learning. A lifelong learning society requires the learner to be at the center and to accommodate to diverse body of learners' needs. In doing so, the form of education has an emphasis on the motivation to learn, and providing a self-paced and self-directed online learning. Consequently, open learning program are increasingly becoming an essential model of learning for lifelong learners and as such there has been fast growth in the number of open learning programs. It is essential for educators and administrators to provide effective online guidance services as a part of their educational programs with the increasing number of open learning programs continue to grow (Zhang & Ng, 2006). It is essential to understand the processes of what constitutes open education.

Higher education has become the next big movement for nations. The public policy focus on higher education reflects a growing consensus in the macroeconomics development. Knowledge about technology and levels of information flow are now considered critical for economic development and account for differential growth patterns. Universities are viewed as key drivers to the knowledge economy. As a result, higher education institutions have been encouraged to develop links with industry and business in a series of new venture partnerships. This emphasis in higher education policy also accords with initiatives to promote greater entrepreneurial skills and activity within national systems of innovation (Peters, 2003). It is through many aspects of open education that it will create new opportunities for students, educators, and administrators.

The global economy is rapidly changing how individuals, businesses, and governments relate. The world's balance of economic power has shifted since the beginning of the 21st Century. Globalization increases the speed at which goods and services move across international borders, and poses challenges, as well as opportunities, for many segments of the economy. As corporations begin to become global, they not only affect regional cultures, but also breed hostility in countries where dissatisfied citizens are taking anti-globalization and anti-democratic actions to preserve their traditional cultures, values, and traditions. The changes brought by corporate globalization are viewed by others as a vehicle for the advancement of capitalism, democracy, economic development, and personal freedoms around the world. As more workers are discontented by globalization, governments and public officials assume greater responsibilities for ensuring education improvements and economic security. Globalization is having a significant impact on the roles and responsibilities of business, government, and society (Milakovich, 2006).

In our world economy there are requirements and demands for rules in international business. The international business community petitions governments to enforce agreements that promote order and openness. A large number of these agreements are global because the support of both developed and developing nations are needed for their effectiveness. The United Nations organizations serve the economic interests of developing nations by assisting in their ability to influence governments. The economic legal framework of international association is designed to provide a proper organization and conduct cooperation agreements. The regulatory features of the economic and legal framework of the international relationship play an important role which ensures a successful organization. The economic and legal structure of the international relationship is considered a concrete and immediate. This provides countries the opportunities which are more favorable with the hopes of gaining the benefits by maintaining and expanding economic relations (Zamfir, 2009).

An essential element economic globalization is developing economic relations. The economic system involves nation states, as trading partners, with the goal to achieve trade, economic cooperation, and participation at the international division of labor. The agreements have played a key role in fostering free trade. These trade agreements promote fair competition and encourage governments to adopt open and transparent rulemaking processes and non-discriminatory laws and regulations. Trade agreements can strengthen the business environment by including commitments on issues of concern along with the reduction and elimination of tariffs. Bilateral, multilateral, and regional trade agreements strongly affect individuals at all levels by the regulation of prices, tariffs, and exports (Zamfir, 2009).

Society and industry are increasingly more dependent on innovation in the areas ranging from science to entertainment. Shared knowledge evolves and is always changing because of the continuous questioning by the participants and is improved through the combined efforts of its contributors. Complex thinking can be the result of collective shared knowledge with the outcomes for individuals being able to share ideas and knowledge freely having the ability to achieve the best possible results (Nelson, Christopher, & Mims, 2009).

One of the many roles of educational institutions in a nation's economy is to increase its ability to transfer research to industry, generate new inventions and patents, and spin-off its technology. "Openness has become a leading source of innovation in the world global digital economy, increasingly adopted by world governments, international agencies, and multinationals, as well as by leading educational institutions as a means of promoting scientific inquiry and international collaboration" (Peters, 2009, p. 203).

Openness can be a driving force to knowledge creation and social and economic advancement through the development of a knowledge society. Openness is increasingly receiving high degrees of attention from scholars, professionals and policy makers in recent years. A growing number of publications and conferences are exploring these subjects from various angles. Openness is becoming essential to ideas in the growing area of policy development in higher education. Technology frequently changes a culture's norms and requires societies to stay current in the evolving culture. Some faculty and administrators believe by simply providing reasonable hi-tech infrastructures is all that is required to develop and maintain effective technological pedagogy. It is essential for educational systems to provide opportunities for students to develop practical and cognitive skills (Langer & Knefelkamp, 2008).

ECONOMICS OF EDUCATION

The economics of education is a struggle that needs to be addressed in relation to knowledge production and ownership. With the emergence of an economics of information, in which information is treated simultaneously as an object of consumption, productive element, commercial signal, and much more. This opens up a potentially bewildering new prospect to scholars, due in particular to the not inconsiderable differences that exist between the economics of ideas and the economics of things (Romello & Silva, 2006). Intellectual property rights (IPR) reform has been underway since the 1990s and actively pursued by most developing countries after the World Trade Organization's (WTO) Agreement on Trade Related Aspects of Intellectual Property Rights (TRIPS) came into effect in 1995. Under the terms of TRIPS, current and future members of WTO must adopt and enforce strong non-discriminatory minimum standards of intellectual property protection in each of the areas commonly associated with IPRs including patents, copyrights, trademarks, and trade secrets (Adams, 2010).

Christopher May suggests to continue or even expand control over information through commoditization and digital rights management has hindered openness. Intellectual Property is never going away, but a social balance is being re-established between property and openness. These are not unconnected or separate ideas, but rather encompass a range of political positions about how we should value and exchange knowledge and information (May, 2008). Beyond strengthening of IPR, the TRIPS Agreement is the first multilateral trade accord that aims at achieving partial harmonization in an extensive area of business regulation, as it seeks to establish deep integration of domestic regulatory policies across countries. IPR has therefore become part of the infrastructure supporting investments in research and development that are important in innovation. The creation of an effective IPR has created an incentive for new knowledge creation and its dissemination (Adams, 2010). A country that enhances its IPR may attract additional knowledge intensive products, which will otherwise be unavailable on the local market and international technology transfer is likely to occur (Lippoldt, 2006). Developing countries are likely to benefit from the reform of their intellectual property system (Adams, 2010).

The internet has made a challenging impact on the structure of relatively fragile societies and touch on cultural sensitivities. This has been recognized by the World Trade Organization (WTO) in the development of the General Agreement on Trade in Services (GATS). The WTO notes that the Internet is making important contributions to recent changes in higher education, by improving existing forms and structures of tertiary education and by introducing changes to the processes and organization of higher education. In addition, available sources emphasize the emergence of innovative institutional arrangements between public and private entities, both within and across national boundaries (Farrington, 2001).

For these reasons, the WTO is interested in liberalizing trade in educational services, as defined by reference to the International Standard Classification of Education, 1997 (ISCED). This is potentially big business, particularly in the USA, which is pro-active in the area, seeing potential markets in management and technical training and skills upgrading, to produce a workforce that is technologically aware. Recent communications to WTO from the EU make no specific reference to education services provided by electronic means. Some countries limit recognition of private institutions and the movement of non-EU persons to take up employment in higher education. It may be argued that EU countries should take a stance similar to the US in relation to this trade, which will otherwise be dominated by the US (Farrington, 2001).

Economic, political, and social forces shape intellectual property policies and practices at colleges and universities. Although each force by itself plays a role in shaping colleges' and universities' policies toward intellectual property, these forces represent the bigger environmental conditions that affect the legal structures, technological advancements, and competing interests that shape the policies and practices in higher education. Intellectual property rights, during the information age, addressed the issues of the public good. The cost of creation is high, but the cost of reproduction is low, and that once the work is created it may be easily reproduced without depleting the original creation. Intellectual property security is necessary to ensure that the creator has an economic incentive to create works that will benefit the public (ASHE, 2008).

Intellectual property rights, particularly during the information age, purportedly address what is usually understood as the "public good problem." The cost of creation is high, but the cost of reproduction is low, and that once the work is created it may be easily reproduced without depleting the original creation. Intellectual property protection is necessary to ensure that the creator has an economic incentive to create works that will benefit the public. Consequently, technology makes creations initially expensive, but expansive and reproduction easy at a substantially lower cost, the legal history of intellectual properties in the United States has been one of access and use, balanced with incentives and rewards (ASHE, 2008).

Intellectual goods that are unprotected by intellectual property may still be protected directly or indirectly by other legal devices, which includes technology.

If these alternative means can substitute the capacities provided by intellectual property rights, then legal changes have no effect. If these alternative means can match or exceed the capacities provided by intellectual property rights, then legal changes that expand these rights have no substantial net effect (Barnett, 2009).

Theoretical Concept

Globalization, advances in information technology, and increasing Internet usage are creating developments in property rights issues that need to be addressed by not only researchers, but also managers and public policy makers. For example, the tens of thousands of computer programmers that make up the "Open Source" community built the famous Linux operating system, which is free, dependable, and owned by no one. The common thread in these examples is that they all raise questions related to the level of definition of property rights over knowledge-based resources, which can range from specific technical, functional, and creative skills to secondary resources created via the use of such skills (Costello & Costello, 2005).

Whether or not a valuable resource can remain in the public domain depends on the costs versus the benefits of defining property rights. Many knowledge-based resources are subject to positive network externalities. Resources become more valuable to users as the number of consumers using those increases. This increase in value stems from benefits such as interchangeability of complementary products, ease of communication between parties using the same product, and cost savings via standardization. For many knowledge-based resources, there may be costs of reduced investment if property rights are defined too well. For example, biotechnology is an industry in which the costs of creating new products are very high and the costs of reverse-engineering a product once it is created are relatively low (Costello & Costello, 2005).

Many regard widening access to intellectual property to be part of the democratization of leisure and the progress of civil society. By widening access through transferring intellectual property on to the net, the participation by people who have been previously excluded or restricted on property grounds is increased. The production and consumption of intellectual property involves an exchange relationship measured in terms of money. It is precisely this relationship that is changed by deregulation and P2P technology. In the context of globalization, P2P sharing permits those sections of the world's population who are disadvantaged access to economic resources with which to enrich their leisure experience and widen participation in global consumer culture (Rojek, 2005).

The creative commons approach is about balancing the copyright structure. The ability to maintain protection on the one hand while also allowing the greater distribution of ideas on the other. In the creative commons its desired outcomes is to achieve a balance between the different degrees of control of knowledge and information, which can lead to greater creativity and innovation. All of the commons licenses allow file sharing provided it is not for monetary gain, if this is the case then the license must be one which has not got a non-commercial use attached. It is suggested that this system of the creative commons allows for increased access to material and thus allows creativity to flourish. The commercial use can be made of the work and so the financial incentives are also (Geach, 2009).

The success of adopting a wide scale commons approach is dependent on whether the potential for commercial incentives is convincing enough for the industry and the government. By allowing the widespread distribution of content without controls, a wider market can be created for that content through increased awareness and interest. When producing new content a producer can use the work of others as inspiration or as a starting point, helping to reduce the production costs. This course of action is in gaining growing commercial acceptance as a method of adding economic value to a business (Geach, 2009).

An important lesson for developing economies is that copyright protection can have both positive and negative effects on creativity. For economic development, copyright policy must be structured so that creators have sufficient protection against copyright infringement, the anticipation which would tend to discourage creators from investing in their work. Economic development protection must also rest on ongoing creativity, so that copyright protection must not be too strong as to shelter copy right owners from competition in the marketplace. Copyright protection and enforcement require granting of permission to access works and the payment of licensing fees and royalties, and can raise the price of copyrighted works by increasing the cost of provision. The technological development in developing countries will be hampered if access to the knowledge base of society is more costly (Park, 2010).

At the same time, the copyright system may enable a greater variety of creative works than would otherwise be available without copyright laws. The increased flow of new knowledge could balance the higher cost of accessing existing knowledge. For copyright laws to be conducive to economic development, copyrighted creations must diffuse widely. The technological development of developing nations will be hampered if access to the knowledge base of society is more costly. The increased flow of new knowledge could offset the higher cost of accessing existing knowledge. The protection of copyrighted works serves not only the interests of copyright owners in industrialized countries, but also those in developing countries. The cost of copyright protection is likely to be higher in developing countries. Their levels of income and wealth are lower, so royalties and licensing payments are more burdensome to creators in developing countries (Park, 2010).

Intellectual Property

Although relationships between university and industry are not a new phenomenon, the context which characterized the 1980s and early 1990s favored their institutionalization. This institutionalization was characterized by the creation of technology transfer offices the review of university missions, and the standardization of contracts, patent support and the development of public relations strategies (Crespo & Dridi, 2007).

There is a vast literature on university and industry relationships. Studies have shown that universities are interested in partnerships with industry because of shrinking public funds. Before the long standing trend in reducing funds, universities had established partnerships with the private sector. This is the case, in particular, of Land Grant universities in the United States and of certain private universities such as MIT and Stanford. However, the scale and the nature of university–industry partnerships beginning in the 1980s distinguish them from earlier collaborations.

In light of this change, Rhoades and Slaughter (2004) argue that we are witnessing a shift in knowledge/learning regimes. They give evidence that knowledge and learning in Academia which was considered largely as a public good, have become much more utilitarian and commercially oriented. They call this new regime the "academic capitalist knowledge/learning regime." The authors note that the two regimes can, and in fact do coexist in universities. In this new regime, academic managers, professors and other professionals are actors who initiate academic capitalism and are not simply absorbed by market pressures or, as they put it "just players being 'corporatized'" (Rhoades & Slaughter, 2004, p. 12).

IP is a form of intangible property, though it is likely being embodied in a palpable entity that is transferred from the originator to another person. It is often said that the protection of IP is the protection of ideas, but ideas are unlike other property in that, when the originator passes the idea to a second party, both can enjoy its benefits; in the absence of restraints, the second party can pass the idea to yet others. To be effective, an IP protection system must allow purchasers to obtain the benefit of the idea through its use and/or title to its physical embodiment, while the IP owner retains the power to prohibit that buyer, and all other parties, from copying or otherwise commercially exploiting the idea embodied in the product (Mittelstaedt & Mittelstaedt, 1997).

Intellectual property has emerged as a major issue, both inside and outside the university community. The debate surrounding intellectual property revolves around issues related to academic identity and culture and whether university–industry relationships pose a threat. With the intensification of these relationships, so, too, has this debate intensified. To cope with this threat, universities have created technology transfer offices with a view to regulating intellectual property generated by researchers. All private-sector contracts with university researchers have to go through these offices (Crespo & Dridi, 2007). The intensification of university–industry relations requires specific expertise related to patent protection. To obtain a patent, the discovery in question must not have been previously disclosed either by the author of by other persons. Most countries have a complete newness policy, according to which a patent is granted only if the invention has not been publicly known anywhere in the world. In the United States, confidential disclosure to a technology transfer office, for example, is important because it is the moment when a discovery is confidentially disclosed and not the moment of patent demanding that counts for protecting intellectual property (Crespo & Dridi, 2007).

Intellectual property has become essential to higher education because of economic, political, and social forces making knowledge and research serve as central commodities. Since ideas and expressions translate into commodities, the environmental pressure over the treatment of intellectual property at colleges and universities changed. Current economic trends make consideration of intellectual property imperative to the broader understanding of the forces that shape the treatment of creations and discoveries derived in and from institutions of higher education. The increasing importance of intellectual property is largely attributable to the shift that moved the United States and other nation-states from an industrial society to an "information society." "Information society" refers to economies in which control over knowledge has replaced control over matter as the ultimate source of economic power (ASHE, 2008).

Intellectual property is essential to economies based on information or knowledge. In the information age, ideas and expressions become commodities, and universities must contend with the legal parameters. The economic health of nations and corporations is determined largely by their ability to develop, commercialize, and exploit scientific and technological innovations and intellectual property rights are the legal means to protect the investment in innovation. As organizations use knowledge as the catalyst to increase the values of their products and services, they seek to capture such knowledge for their exclusive control. Knowledge, once feeding the productive processes and services of these corporations, now is itself deemed property. Once knowledge is deemed property, intellectual property laws become central to the economy (May, 2000).

If we understand intellectual property as a distributive instrument, then intellectual property may matter as an incentive that operates primarily and indirectly at the "macro" level of industrial organization. If intellectual property supports the economic feasibility of structures it may also develop innovation investment to which such structures are well-suited. While further inquiry is certainly required, there is limited, but meaningful evidence that individuals, universities, business, and organization demonstrate a unique understanding of the innovation cycle (Barnett, 2009).

As to no surprise, the complexities of dealing with intellectual property in the information age have become more pressing in higher education. Higher education now operates under a different context, one in which colleges and universities regularly contend with numerous legal questions about the nature and scope of intellectual property. It is a matter of time and patience for the legal and innovative structures to work in tandem to ensure IP protection and knowledge transfer to benefit our global society.

REFERENCES

Adams, S. (2010). Intellectual property rights, investment climate and FDI in developing countries. *International Business Research, 3*(3), 201–209.
ASHE (2008). Overview of intellectual property. *ASHE Higher Education Report, 34*(4), 1–12.

Ausburn, L. J. (2004). Course design elements most valued by adult learners in blended online education environments: An american perspective. *Educational Media International, 41*(4), p. 327–337.

Barnett, J. B. (2009). Is intellectual property trivial? *University of Pennsylvania Law Review, 157,* 1691–1742.

Costello, A. O. & Costello, T. G. (2005). Defining Property Rights: The case of knowledge based resources. *California Management Review, 7*(3), 143–155.

Crespo, M. & Dridi, H. (2007). Intensification of university–industry relationships and its impact on academic research. *High Education, 54,* 61–84.

Farrington, D. J. (2001). Borderless higher education: Challenges to regulation, accreditation, and intellectual property rights. *Minerva,* 63–84.

Geach, N. (2009). The future of copyright in the age of convergence: Is a new approach needed for the new media world? International Review of Law, Computers & Technology, *23*(1–2), 131–142.

ISCED (1997). International standard classification of education. UNESCO. p. 1–48.

Langer, A. M. & L. Lee Knefelkamp. L. L. (2008). College students' technology arc: A model for understanding progress. *Theory Into Practice, 47,* 186–196.

Lippoldt, D. (2006). Intellectual property rights, pharmaceuticals and foreign direct investment. *Group d'Economie Mondale de Sciences Po.* 1–10.

May, C. (2008). The world intellectual property organization and the development agenda. *Global Society, 22*(1), p. 97–113.

May, C. (2009). Globalizing the logic of openness: Open source software and the global governance of intellectual property. (Chadwick, A. & Howard, P. N. eds). Internet Politics 364–375. New York: Routledge.

Milakovich, M. E. (2006). *Improving Service Quality in the Global Economy.* Boca Raton, Florida: Auerbach Publishers.

Mittelstaedt, J. D. & Mittelstaedt, R. A. (1997). The protection of intellectual property: Issues of origination and ownership. *Journal of Public Policy & Marketing. 16*(1) 14–25.

Nelson, J., Christopher, A. & Mims, C. (2009). Tpack and web 2.0: Transformation of Teaching and Learning. *TechTrends, 53*(5), 80–87.

Park, W. G. (2010). The copyright dilemma: Copyright systems, innovation and economic development. *Journal of International Affairs, 64*(1), 53.

Peters, M. A. (2003). Globalisation, societies and education, classical political economy and the ole of universities in the new knowledge economy. *1*(2), 153–168.

Peters, M.A. (2009). Open education and the open science economy. Globalization and the Study of Education (Popkewitz, T. & Rizvi, F., eds).

Ramello, G. B. & Silva, F. (2006). Appropriating signs and meaning: The elusive economics of trademark. Industrial and Corporate Change, *15*(6), 937–963.

Rhoades, G. & Slaughter, S. (2004). Academic capitalism in the new economy: Challenges and choices. American Academic, *1*(1), 37–59.

Rojek, C. (2005). P2P leisure exchange: Net banditry and the policing of intellectual property. *Leisure Studies, 24*(4), 357–369.

Zamfir, B. (2009). The economic and legal framework of the international relations: A conceptual approach. *Young Economists Journal / Revista Tinerilor Economisti, 7,* 134–143.

Zhang, W. & Ng, T.K. (2006). Distance guidance for lifelong learners in Hong Kong: development of an online programme preference assessment instrument. *International Journal of Lifelong Education, 25*(6), 633–644.

KNOWLEDGE SOCIALISM AND UNIVERSITIES: INTELLECTUAL COMMONS AND OPPORTUNITIES FOR 'OPENNESS' IN THE 21ST CENTURY WITH GARETT GIETZEN

INTRODUCTION

'Openness' is a central contested value of modern liberalism that falls under different political, epistemological and ethical descriptions. In this chapter, we employ 'openness' to analyze the spatialization of learning and education. We discuss dimensions of openness and 'open education' (Peters & Britez, 2008), beginning with a brief history of openness in education that focuses on the concept of the Open University as it first developed in the United Kingdom during the 1960s, a development we dub Open University 1.0. We then consider the concept of openness in the light of the new 'technologies of openness' of Web 2.0 that promote interactivity and encourage participation, collaboration and help to establish new forms of the intellectual commons, a space for knowledge sharing and collective work The intellectual commons is increasingly based on models of open source, open access, open archives, open journal systems and open education. We call this model Open University 2.0. Where the former is based on the logic of centralized industrial media characterized by a broadcast one-to-many mode, the latter is based upon a radically decentralized, many-to-many and peer production mode of interactivity. To exemplify the progress and possibilities of Open University 2.0, we focus on MIT's OpenCourseWare and Harvard's open access initiative to publicly post its faculty's papers online. Finally, we look forward to the possibilities of a form of openness that combines the benefits of these first two forms, what we call Open University 3.0, and consider its possibilities for universities in the future. By doing so, we see this chapter as a means to investigate the political economy of openness as it reconfigures universities in the knowledge economy of the 21st century and at the same time to suggest a socialized model of the knowledge economy that competes with neoliberal versions.

The underlying argument of the chapter focuses upon the ways in which new forms of technological-enabled openness, especially emergent social media that utilizes social networking, blogs, wikis and user-created content and media, provide new models of openness for a conception of the intellectual commons based on peer production which is a radically decentralized, genuinely interactive, and collaborative form of knowledge sharing that can usefully serve as the basis of 'knowledge cultures' (Peters & Besley, 2006; Peters & Roberts, 2010). Openness 1.0 was based on social democratic principles that emphasized inclusiveness and equality of opportunity and was a product of the age of welfarism when higher education was seen as an unqualified public good yet the mechanism of Openness 1.0 followed that of industrial broadcast mass media, which was designed to reach a large audience on a one-to-many logic. In one sense the technology contradicted the social democratic values permitting only a one-way transfer of knowledge. Openness 2.0 is based on what might be called principles of liberal political economy, particularly intellectual property and freedom of information. This second iteration of openness employs new P2P architectures and technologies that are part of the ideology of Web 2.0 and given expression in ways that emphasize the ethic of participation ('participatory media'), collaboration and file-sharing characterizing the rise of social media that is interactive and collaboartive.

We argue that Open University 2.0 provides the basis for a new social media model of the university that embraces the social democratic articles of the original Open University and that it provides the means to recover and enhance the historical mission of the university in the twenty-first century (Peters, 2006). Open University 2.0 provides mechanisms for jettisoning the dominant neoliberal managerialist ideology and returning to a fully socialized view of knowledge and knowledge-sharing that has its roots in Enlightenment thinking about science and its new practices in commons-based peer-production. This position relies on the argument that knowledge and education are fundamental social activities and that knowledge and the value of knowledge are fundamentally rooted in social relations (Peters & Besley, 2006). At the same time, however, we recognize that any re-theorization of the university must move beyond the limitations of even Open University 2.0, which – despite its logic of openness – often coheres around exclusive institutions such as MIT and Harvard and is correspondingly reliant on factors of exclusivity, including intellectual property and the privileging of 'expertise'. Consequently, the development of openness as it relates to the university must move from the social democratic model of Open University 1.0, and the liberal political economy model of Open University 2.0, to a new version of openness based on 'knowledge socialism'. Only through such a development might this new Open University 3.0 achieve its potential as a locus of true inclusion and social and economic creativity.

MEDIA AND EDUCATION: THE PROMISE OF WEB 2.0

With Web 2.0, there is a deep transformation occurring wherein the Web has become a truly participatory media; instead of going on the Web to read static content, we can more easily create and share our own ideas and creations. The rise of what has been alternately referred to as consumer- or user-generated media (content) has been hailed as being truly groundbreaking in nature. Blogging and social networking with the facility of user-generated content has created revolutionary new social media that characterize Web 2.0 as the newest phase of the Internet. New interactive technologies and peer-to-peer architectures have democratized writing and imaging and, thereby, the conditions for creativity itself, enabling anyone with computer access to become a creator of their own digital content. Writers and video-makers as 'content creators' are causing a fundamental shift from the age of information to the age of interaction and recreating themselves in the process. Sometimes this contrast is given in terms of a distinction between 'industrial media', 'broadcast' or 'mass' media which is highly centralized, hierarchical and vertical based on one-to-many logic versus social media which is decentralized (without a central server), non-hierarchical or peer-governed, and horizontal based on many-to-many interaction.

Forms of industrial mass media including the book, newspapers, radio, television, film and video broadcast media were designed to reach very large audiences within the industrializing nation-state. The major disadvantage of this media form is the criticism of manipulation, bias and ideology that comes with a one-to-many dissemination, its commodification of information, and its corporate method of production and distribution (Thompson, 1995). Mass media communication is a one-way transmission model where the audience is reduced to a passive consumer of programmed information which is suited to mass audiences. Both industrial and social media provide the scalable means for reaching global audiences. The means of production for industrial media are typically owned privately or by the state and require specialized technical expertise to produce and payment to access. Social media, by contrast, is based on the Internet as platform, and tend to be available free or at little cost, requiring little or no technical operating knowledge. There are also profound differences in production and consumption processes, in the immediacy of the two types of media and in the levels and means of participation and reception.

Even so it is not a question of straightforward replacement. Many of the industrial media are rapidly adopting aspects of social media to develop more interactive capacity. CNN, for instance, has introduced its blogs with viewer participation and interaction and encourage viewers to follow stories on Twitter and Facebook. This means that new media will not simply replace old media, but rather will learn to interact with it in a complex relationship Bolter and Grusin (2001) calls 'remediation' and Henry Jenkins (2006) calls 'convergence culture'. Jenkins argues that convergence culture is not primarily a technological revolution but is more a cultural shift, dependent on the active participation of the consumers working in a social dynamic. Douglas Kellner and George Kim (2009) theorize YouTube as the cutting edge of ICTs and characterize it as dialogical learning community, and for learning-by-doing, learning as communication, learning through reflection on the environment, learning as self-fulfillment and empowerment, learning for agency and social change.

We accept the idea that the advances in information and communication technologies provides the means to expand the community of higher education beyond the traditional campus, creating opportunities for increased openness in access to education. Rather than using the terminology from software development, however, we wish to ground the definition of this openness within the tradition of critical spatiality. Through doing so, we will problematize the notion that the campus is the natural boundary of the higher education experience – a notion which inherently perpetuates pedagogies of inequality and elitism – and suggest that openness offers a new critical relationship between advanced learning and the community beyond the walls of the college.

The socially networked universe has changed the material conditions for the formation, circulation, and utilization of knowledge. 'Learning' has been transformed from its formal mode under the industrial economy, structured through class, gender and age to an informal and ubiquitous mode of learning 'any where, anytime' in the information and media-based economy. Increasingly, the emphasis falls on the 'learning economy,' improving learning systems and networks, and the acquisition of new media literacies. These mega-trends signal changes in both the production and consumption of symbolic goods and their situated contexts of use. The new media logics accent the 'learner's' *co-production* and the active production of meaning in a variety of networked public and private spaces, where knowledge and learning emerge as new principles of social stratification, social mobility and identity formation.

New media technologies not only diminish the effect of distance but they also thereby conflate the local and the global, the private and the public, 'work' and 'home'. They spatialize knowledge systems. Digitalization of learning systems increases the speed, circulation and exchange of knowledge highlighting the importance of digital representations of all symbolic and cultural resources, digital cultural archives, and *new literacies and models of text management, text distribution and generation.* At the same time, the radical concordances of image, text and sound, and the development of global information/knowledge infrastructures have created new learning opportunities while encouraging the emergence of a global media network linked with a global communications network together with the emergence a global Euro-American consumer culture and the rise of *global edutainment* media conglomerates, where education is reduced to the principles of entertainment. In the media economy the political economy of ownership become central; who owns and designs learning systems becomes a question of paramount political and philosophical significance.

New models of flexible learning nest within new technologies that are part of wider historical emerging techno-capitalist systems that promote greater interconnectivity and encompass all of its different modes characterizing communication from the telegraph (city-to-city), the media (one-to-many), the telephone (one-on-one), the Internet (one-to-one, one-to-all, all-to-one, all-to-all, many-to-many, etc.), the World Wide Web (collective by content but connective by access), the mobile/cell phone (all the interconnectivity modes afforded by the web and internet, plus a body-to-body connection). At the same time these new affordances seem to provide new opportunities for learning that reflect old social democratic goals concerning equality, access and emancipation that made education central to both liberal and socialist ideals.

OPEN UNIVERSITY 1.0

Well before the emergence of the Internet and the phenomenon of social networking appeared in the mid 1990s, the model of the 'open university' in the United Kingdom was established as a technology-based distance education institution in the 1960s. The Open University was founded on the idea that communications technology could extend advanced degree learning to those people who for a variety of reasons could not easily attend campus universities. The Open University really began when in 1923 the educationalist J. C. Stobart while working for the infant BBC wrote a memo suggesting that the new communications and broadcast media could develop a 'wireless university'. By the early sixties many different ideas were being proposed including a 'teleuniversity' that would broadcast lectures, as well as providing correspondence texts and organizing campus visits to local universities.

Yet the Open University was not merely an institution that followed from the development of technical mechanisms of openness. From the start the idea of the 'open university' was conceived, in social democratic terms, as a response to the problem of exclusion. Michael Young (Baron Young of Dartington, 1915–2002), the sociologist, activist and politician, who first coined the term and helped found the Open University, wrote the 1945 manifesto for the Labor Party under Clement Atlee and devoted himself to social reform of institutions based on their greater democratization and giving the people a stronger role in their governance.[1]

A Labor Party study group under the chairmanship of Lord Taylor presented a report in March 1963 concerning the continuing exclusion from higher education of the lower income groups and they proposed a 'University of the Air' as an experiment for adult education. The Open University was established in Milton Keynes in September1969 with Professor Walter Perry as its first Vice-Chancellor. It took its first cohort of students in 1970 which began foundation courses in January 1971. The 1980s was a decade of growth and consolidation. As the OU website notes 'By 1980, total student numbers had reached 70,000, and some 6,000 people were graduating each year. From then on the institution would each year boost new records in the numbers of people applying to study and achieving their degree.'[2] During the 1980s and 1990s new faculties of business, management, languages and law were added and the OU expanded into Europe attracting more than 10,000 EU citizens outside the UK. Today the OU has some 180,000 students in the UK (150,000 undergraduate and more than 30,000 postgraduate students) with an additional 25,000 overseas students making it one of the largest universities in the world. Over 10,000 students attending OU have disabilities.

The Open University[3] advertises itself as based on 'open learning' which is explained in terms of 'learning in your own time by reading course material, working on course activities, writing assignments and perhaps working with other students.' It has been immensely influential as a model for other countries and distance education flourished in the 1970s and picked up new open education dimensions with the introduction of local area network environments.[4] The mission of the OU is stated as:

> The Open University is open to people, places, methods and ideas. It promotes educational opportunity and social justice by providing high-quality university education to all who wish to realise their ambitions and fulfill their potential. Through academic research, pedagogic innovation and collaborative partnership, it seeks to be a world leader in the design, content and delivery of supported open and distance learning. (http://www.open.ac.uk/about/ou/p2.shtml)

The OU is explicit in its commitment to equality and diversity:

- Our mission expresses our founding aspiration to provide opportunities to all. As such, equality and diversity have been part of the core values of the Open University since its inception.
- Our continued dedication to social justice and equality of opportunity is embodied in a set of commitments and principles. Through these commitments, we will strengthen our position as a university of choice.

Today there are some 43 open universities in the world based on the British model.[5]

TOWARDS OPEN UNIVERSITY 2.0

MIT's OpenCourseWare 2000

According to MIT, OpenCourseWare (OCW) developed from a consideration of how the Internet might be used to further MIT's mission "to advance knowledge and to educate students". (http://ocw.mit.edu/about/our-history/) MIT anticipated a revenue-generating initiative but exploration led to a different type of program. (Abelson, 2008) Officially proposed in 2000, OCW furthers MIT's mission by providing free worldwide access to the "core academic content" of its undergraduate and graduate courses, including syllabi, lecture notes, assignments, exams, and audio and video media. The pilot version of OpenCourseWare went on-line in 2002 with content from 50 courses, including Spanish and Portuguese translations. In 2007, it was launched officially with 500 courses, which expanded to 1,800 courses by 2007. 33 disciplines and nearly all of MIT's curricula are represented, not only engineering and other technical areas, but also the humanities, management and the natural and social sciences. By 2009, OCW had expanded to over 1,900 courses and additional translations into Chinese, Persian and Thai. (http://ocw.mit.edu/about/our-history/) [6]

As of October 2009, MIT recorded 86.8 million visits to OpenCourseWare, an average of one million visits each month. Visitors access OCW directly and via 220 mirror sites around the world. 46% of traffic is from the United States, 17% from East Asia, 11% from Western Europe, 9% from South Asia, 4% from Latin

America, and the remaining 13% from other parts of the world. (2009 Program Evaluation Findings Summary) Visits are differentiated into four user types: 9% are identified as educators, 42% as students, 43% as self-learners and the remaining 6% as other types. (http://ocw.mit.edu/OcwWeb/web/about/stats/index.htm). The educators, students and self-learners who comprise the majority of users identify a range of reasons for accessing OCW:

- Educator uses: enhanced personal knowledge (45%), learning new teaching methods (15%), incorporating OCW materials into teaching materials (14%)
- Student uses: enhancing personal knowledge (44%), complementing a course (39%), planning a course of study (12%)
- Self learner uses: exploring interests outside of professional field (41%), planning future study (20%), reviewing basic concepts in field (17%), keeping current in field (11%). (2009 Program Evaluation Findings Summary)

This considerable use demonstrates OCW's significant impact, which is further substantiated by personal testimonials by users of course materials and MIT faculty and administrators.[7] It is clear that OpenCourseWare addresses a wide range of educational needs. It makes academic content accessible to people who might otherwise be denied due to a wide range of factors, including geography, poverty and time or other logistical limitations. It allows MIT to promote knowledge sharing in meaningful ways, thus serving the ideals of openness through the affordances of technology. As former MIT President Charles Vest observed in 2001, OpenCourseWare "combines two things: the traditional openness and outreach and democratizing influence of American education and the ability of the Web to make vast amounts of information instantly available." (http://web.mit.edu/newsoffice/2001/ocw.html).

As impressive as MIT OpenCourseWare may be, MIT makes it explicitly clear that it is "not an MIT education." OCW "does not grant degrees or certificates" or "provide access to MIT faculty"; and the materials provided "may not reflect entire content of the course." (http://ocw.mit.edu/OcwWeb/web/about/about/index.htm) It only provides access to "core academic content", not the university itself. Faculty at other institutions may employ it in their own work, and students and autodictats may use it to learn subject matter of MIT courses, and but neither of these options are the same as real access to MIT. OpenCourseWare does indeed share with the university a role in disseminating knowledge; and like the university, it serves teaching, learning and research. The extent to which OCW can fulfill these roles is limited because it does not provide direct access to faculty who would facilitate the learning process to students, self-learners and other educators, and nor does it provide the infrastructure necessary to most types of research, especially in the sciences. Nevertheless, OCW can indeed make claims in these areas, albeit limited ones.

However, the university is more than a teaching, learning and research mechanism, it also provides credentials that certify skills and legitimate graduates in the job market and professions. These credentials demonstrate that graduates attended a particular institution and therefore accrued cultural capital that provides benefits ostensibly unrelated to employment skills, especially in the social realm.[8] This role in legitimation and cultural capital accrual extends to the teaching and research faculty, which can claim institutional affiliation.

Hence despite that fact that MIT, in calling its initiative "open", is drawing on the terminology of the open-source software movement, it does not, in any profound sense, open the University to those who do not otherwise have access to it. Rather, like open-source software itself, OCW replicates existing patterns of knowledge production in academia and reaffirm the closed relationship of the university community to the world at large. That said, by providing free access to knowledge, it does' indeed adhere to some liberal ideals, including scientific knowledge sharing ideals that developed during the Enlightenment. OCM has a great deal of similarities with the UK's Open University, an example of what we are describing as "Open University 1.0." *That* Open University relied on technologies to bridge distance and by doing so increase inclusion. OpenCourseWare relies on today's far more sophisticated technologies, as well as the attraction of free content which is accessible to all regardless of academic background, to reach a greater number of people. In this respect, OpenCourseWare is even less elitist than the Open University, an institution known for its accessibility. However, the original Open University is differentiated by its ability to provide substantial institutional support to its students and, perhaps more importantly, the legitimating credentials and cultural capital which are accorded its graduates.

OpenCourseWare follows a model with a one-to-many logic that has more in common with Open University 1.0 than its 2.0 iteration. "Core academic content" travels unidirectionally from the MIT campus to educators, students, self-learners and others around the world. Given the high prestige of MIT among the world's universities, and its geographical location in Cambridge, Massachusetts, also home to Harvard University, the relationship of MIT to the recipients of OpenCourseWare content can be seen as one of centre-periphery. That said, by distributing content worldwide, MIT can also be seen as a mechanism for destabilizing the localization that has traditionally promoted university elitism.

MIT designed the OpenCourseWare model to be replicable, thus facilitating its expansion to other institutions of higher education. (Carson 2009, 26) The legacy of this replicability, the OpenCourseWare Consortium, founded in 2005, now includes member institutions from 36 countries around the world. Spain is the most significantly represented of the top ten countries, with 39 institutions, followed by United States (22), Japan (18), Taiwan (14), South Korea (11), Venezuela (7), Brazil and Saudi Arabia (6), Colombia and United Kingdom (4). Highest institutional concentrations are in Asia, Europe, and Latin and North America; Africa is most poorly represented with only one institution. (http://www. ocwconsortium.org/members/consortium-members.html) Like MIT, the Consortium reports a large number of available courses and a high rate of visitor traffic. In a 2008 study, the then 200 members provided more than 6200 courses and over 2.25 million visits per month, not including the traffic generated by more than 1600 courses offered by the China Quality OpenCourseWare program (Carson 2009, 23).

The growth of the OCW Consortium further destabilizes the localization of the traditional university, moving knowledge distribution away from a one-to-many to a many-to-many model. This process moves university development closer to what we have described as Open University 2.0, a model characterized as diffuse and based on a socialized understanding of knowledge and knowledge-sharing. At this point, the OCW Consortium, with MIT OpenCourseWare, have not become a truly interactive and collaborative form of intellectual commons where content is user-created in meaningful ways. Perhaps the university, given its privileging of expert – and legitimated – knowledge cannot accommodate user-created content to the extent possible in other areas, such as entertainment media. Nevertheless, MIT OpenCourseWare and the OCW Consortium are opening greater social, cultural and technical affordances that may, in time, realize the ideals of Open University 2.0.

Harvard's Open Access

Harvard University followed MIT's embrace of openness, but developed a quite different approach. Harvard's creation and implementation of the model of the Open University had its creation with its faculty making their scholarly articles available to everyone while maintaining copyright protection. Harvard became the first university in the U.S. to embrace an Open Access authorization for its faculty. In the creation of the policy, the faculty was concerned that there could be copyright predicaments and the provisions to maintain ownership of the information was important to some faculty members and the fear was that the policy would control take and would not serve their best collective interests. This Open Access policy and philosophy was faculty-driven which became the first to impose the requirement upon itself instead of having the request coming from the administration. In keeping with the policy/philosophy, faculty members have the right to remove themselves from the contract in which specific cases would be troublesome. The policy requires all faculty members to provide electronic copies of their articles to the Provost's Office (Peek, 2005).

The strength of the policy is that the faculty does not sacrifice anything by sharing the publication rights with Harvard. In doing so, this policy forms a united authority of Harvard if they decide to turn down a journal's request for exclusive publishing rights. Harvard University designed a legal memorandum, which reinforces their negotiations with commercial publishing companies. A distinctive feature of the Open Access policy is that the policy agreement is not coercive from the faculty senate or the university administration. Harvard's Library created a special office that ensures that Open Access information is accessible across the institution's many departments, which contributed to Harvard's goal of a unified institutional atmosphere. A rule in the policy asks the faculty and the administration to review the Open Access policy with the hope of ensuring that everyone who is participating is still content (Peek, 2005).

If other universities choose to follow Harvard's endeavor into Open Access, it will create serious problems for major publishers involved in higher education. The publishing conglomerate Wiley & Sons is composed of sixteen separate publishing houses that deal with education alone. The Open Access policy might create a chain of negative reactions that could force profits to slow. Consequently, the Open Access movement suggests dramatic changes are coming to the journal marketplace. Publishers benefit from the ownership rights that they protect on behalf of both the authors and themselves. Harvard's Open Access policy threatens the traditional traditions of conducting business with scholars and publishing houses. Scholars and researchers have long been willing to sign contracts that provide all copyrights to publishers instead of retaining their own respective rights. With the creation of the Open University 2.0, it will force the scholarly community to break with tradition and require the open sharing of research, software, and data. (Van Orsdel & Born, 2008).

Harvard will continue to have the traditional educational structure of one to one transference of scholarly information. This application of openness allows Harvard and other institutions of higher education to rethink their respective approaches to knowledge and information systems. This new concept of information of a one-to-many method will reshape the scholarly community that currently exists in higher education. Harvard's Open Access to scholarly articles incorporates the fundamental principle of the new technology of openness at it relates to Open University 2.0. The users and distributors of scholarly information may promote collaboration and establish new forms of the intellectual commons (Peters & Besley, 2006; Peters & Roberts, 2010). Harvard's Open Access provides the basis for a new educational framework and challenges the concept of what constitutes a university that embraces the social democratic ideas of the original concept of the Open University 1.0 (Peters, 2006).

This Open Access to large repositories of information creates a new and global university. Harvard's Open Access policy provides a vision of open education, and a possibility for maximizing educational opportunities for individuals. The scholarly collection available through Harvard University provides an opportunity for individual and communal education. Harvard's Open Access policy benefits the independent learners. These learners can be educated in many subjects just by clicking on a link and studying at their leisure. Individuals who have a wide range of educational goals and desires will facilitate the development of educational information by universities. It is because of these diverse interests that the Open Access policy promotes curricular creativity for both the learner and the institution. The learner has the ability to seek and find what is of interest to him or her and learn the information at his or her own pace. While the faculty has, the ability to present their scholarly works in an online format that may be different from their traditional classrooms.

In agreement with MIT's Open Course Ware, the content from the Harvard university courses and degree programs to being a self-directed learner will become a more serious form of education. For the new type/form of learner, institutions will cultivate the emergence of new persons who will become participants in the creation of open education environments. Harvard's Open Access policy helps inaugurate a new type of educator who is part scholar and part information librarian. The quasi scholar-librarian will be concerned with the content of the information that will serve as a way for individuals to be oriented to the appropriate forms of information. In this new educational environment, learning communities will desire to utilize the informational resources, which is available because of the Open Access policy. These quasi scholar-librarians will form new teaching communities not in the traditional sense of scholar to student, but rather having a linear form of sharing valued information. In doing so, the nontraditional classroom environment in which the scholar and student work allows individuals interested to share and submits their own works (Lynch, 2008).

Despite the promise of Harvard's Open Access policy, it shares many of the limitations of MIT's Open Course Ware. As with MIT's initiative, Harvard is changing from an elite and exclusive institution, located in what is arguably the world's most elite academic center, from where it diffuses content in a one-to-many relationship to institutions and individual peripheral learners. Furthermore, the education provided by the reading of faculty articles is informal, undirected and uncredentialled. The factors that may be problematic for some having who have concerns pedagogically, but also educationally is recognized and situated in the educational marketplace.

Yet, as with MIT's Open Course Ware, Harvard's Open Access policy does provide possibilities for bringing Openness 2.0 and the Open University 2.0 to fruition.

Harvard's challenge to a long dominant model of academic publishing promises to benefit all academic institutions by shifting control of knowledge from publishers to the institutions where knowledge is generated. A shift like this might make knowledge more accessible, making it cheaper or even free, but also by undermining the proprietary rights ensured by exclusive information architectures delimited by licensing, passwords, and other mechanisms. The achievement of openness of this sort has the potential to provide academic papers from multiple institutions, in a many-to-many logical framework to people around the world, which facilitates research, scholarship, and learning in truly significant ways.

LOOKING FORWARD: OPENNESS 3.0, OPEN UNIVERSITY 3.0 AND KNOWLEDGE SOCIALISM

The first and second iterations of university openness have provided significant benefits to society. The social democratic character of Openness 1.0 promoted inclusion and opportunity for a wider range of people than would have been traditionally enrolled in university. Knowledge exclusivity was challenged by the institutional assertion that knowledge is a public good. Openness 2.0, with its confluence of freedom of information and technological affordances, further provides a freedom to use, share and improve knowledge. However, both of these forms of openness are necessarily restricted: the first by technical infrastructure limitations, and the latter by resource imbalances and the exclusivity necessary to intellectual property.

The next version of openness, which we call Openness 3.0, combines aspects of the two earlier forms to maximize their respective benefits, while reducing limitations. In this model of openness, education is placed at the center of society and human rights. In this sense, Openness 3.0 shares similarities to Openness 1.0 and its social democratic goals although it is committed to the promotion of forms of free global science, research and learning. At the same time, it also shares with Openness 2.0 a culture of social, ICT-driven knowledge sharing and innovation. However, Openness 3.0 differs because its ideological foundation are not social democratic, nor – like 2.0 – that of liberal political economy. Instead, Openness 3.0 is based on what can be called "knowledge socialism".

Knowledge socialism provides an alternative to the currently dominant "knowledge capitalism". Whereas knowledge capitalism focuses on the economics of knowledge, emphasizing human capital development, intellectual property regimes, and efficiency and profit maximization, knowledge socialism shifts emphasis towards recognition that knowledge and its value are ultimately rooted in social relations (Peters & Besley, 2006). Knowledge socialism promotes the sociality of knowledge by providing mechanisms for a truly free exchange of ideas. Unlike knowledge capitalism, which relies on exclusivity – and thus scarcity – to drive innovation, the socialist alternative recognizes that exclusivity can also greatly limit innovation possibilities (see 'Introduction', Peters et al, 2009). Hence rather than relying on the market to serve as a catalyst for knowledge creation, knowledge socialism marshals public and private financial and administrative resources to advance knowledge for the public good.

Consequently, the university, as a key locus of knowledge creation, becomes – in Openness 3.0 – the mechanism of multiple forms of innovation, not merely in areas with obviously direct economic returns (such as technoscience), but also in those areas (such as information literacy) that facilitate indirect benefits not merely beholden to concern for short-term market gains. Positioning the university in this way might seem overly idealistic, perhaps even disconnected from the tremendous financial realities facing universities, and higher education in general, in much of the world. Reactions of this sort, however, rely on the assumption that the current neoliberal model of higher education, with primacy placed on selling educational "products" to "consumers", is the best remedy to diminishing funding. Furthermore, although individual economic actors maximize personal benefits through their consumption choices, these choices frequently do not correspond to broader societal needs. Free exchange of knowledge in higher education, for instance, does more than provide economic returns to individual actors and institutions. Post-industrial nations, for example, can maximize their place in the global knowledge-based economy by collective, education-based, innovation. Perhaps more importantly, a broader and more social approach to higher education, both in terms of investment and return, provide better means for addressing truly wide-ranging problems such as climate change. The extent to which Openness 3.0, and therefore the Open University 3.0, are practicable remains unclear, but the technical affordances and social needs allow and demand an approach to higher education that moves beyond the limited models remain dominant.

NOTES

[1] See the website of the UA3 at http://www.u3a.org.uk/.
[2] See The History of the Open University at http://www.open.ac.uk/about/ou/p3.shtml on which this section is based.
[3] See http://www.open.ac.uk/.
[4] See, for example, the Indian Open Schooling Network (IOSN) at http://www.nos.org/iosn.htm, the National Institute of Open Schooling at http://www.nos.org/, and Open School BC (British Columbia) at http://www.pss.gov.bc.ca/osbc/.
[5] See http://en.wikipedia.org/wiki/Category:Open_universities.
[6] http://ocw.mit.edu/OcwWeb/web/about/history/index.htm. For a more detailed history of OpenCourseWare, see: Abelson (2008).
[7] See, for instance: "OCW Stories" MIT OpenCourseWare site; and David Diamond, "MIT Everywhere" Wired, November 2009.
[8] "Cultural capital" is introduced in Pierre Bourdieu and Jean-Claude Passeron "Cultural Reproduction and Social Reproduction, 1973" and further articulated in Bourdieu, "The Forms of Capital" (1986).

REFERENCES

2009 Program Evaluation Findings Summary, http://ocw.mit.edu/ans7870/global/ 09_Eval_Summary.pdf
Abelson, H. (2008). The Creation of OpenCourseWare at MIT, *Journal of Science Education and Technology, 17*(2), 164–174.
Bolter, J. D. & Grusin, R. (2001). *Remediation: Understanding New Media.* MIT Press.
Bolter, J.D. & Grusin, R. (2007). *Remediation: Understanding new media.* Cambridge, MA.: MIT Press.
Carson, S. (2009). The unwalled garden: growth of the OpenCourseWare Consortium, 2001–2008, *Open Learning: The Journal of Open and Distance Learning, 24*(1), 23–29.
Henry, J. (2006). *Convergence Culture: Where Old and New Media Collide.* New York, NY: New York University Press.
Jenkins, H. (2006). Convergence Culture: Where Old and New Media Collide. New York, NYU Press.
Kellner, D. & Kim, G. (2009). YouTube, Politics and Pedagogy. In *Media/Cultural Studies: Critical Approaches* (Eds.) Rhonda Hammer & Douglas Kellner, New York, Peter Lang.
Lynch, C. (2008). Opening Up Education: The Collective Advancement of Education through Open Technology, Open Content, and Open Knowledge. (T. Iivoshi & M.S. V. Kumar, Eds). Cambridge MA: The MIT Press.
Marginson, S., Murphy, P. & Peters, M.A. (2010). *Global Creation: Space, Connection and Universities in the Age of the Knowledge Economy.* New York, Peter Lang.
Murphy, P., Peters, M.A. & Marginson, S. (2010). *Imagination: Three Models of Imagination in the Age of the Knowledge Economy.* New York, Peter Lang.
Peek, R. (2005). RCUK: Free for All. *Information Today, 22*(8), 17–18.
Peters, M. A., Murphy, P. & Marginson, S. (2009). *Creativity and the Global Knowledge Economy.* New York, Peter Lang.
Peters, M. A. & Besley, Tina (A. C.) (2006). *Building Knowledge Cultures: Education and Development in the Age of Knowledge Capitalism.* Lanham, Boulder, NY, Oxford, Rowman & Littlefield.

Peters, M. A. & Britez, R. (2008). (Eds.) *Open Education and Education for Openness.* Rotterdam & Taipei, Sense Publishers.

Peters, M. A. (2006). Derrida and the Question of the Post-Colonial University, *Access: Critical Perspectives on Communication, Cultural & Policy Studies 24*(1–2): 15–25.

Peters, M. A. (2006). Higher Education, Development and the Learning Economy, *Policy Futures in Education, 4*(3): 279-291.

Peters, M. A. (2007). Higher Education, Globalization and The Knowledge Economy: Reclaiming the Cultural Mission, *Ubiquity*, 8, Issue 18, May 8, 2007 – May 14, 2007. At http://www.acm.org/ubiquity/views/v8i18_peter.html. (Reprint).

Peters, M. A. (2007). *Knowledge Economy, Development and the Future of Higher Education.* Rotterdam, Sense Publishers. Thompson, J. (1995). *Media and Modernity.* London, Polity Press.

Thompson, J. B. (1995). *The media and modernity: A social theory of the media.* Palo Alto, CA.: Stanford University Press.

Van Orsdel, L. C. & Born, K. (2008). Embracing Opennes. *Library Journal, 133*(7), 53–58, 6–9 charts.

Young, M. (1958). *The Rise of the Meritocracy.* London, Routledge.

Young, M. & Wilmott, P. (1957). *Family and Kinship in East London.* London, Routledge.

MANAGERIALISM AND THE NEOLIBERAL UNIVERSITY: PROSPECTS FOR NEW FORMS OF 'OPEN MANAGEMENT' IN HIGHER EDUCATION

The learning of one man does not subtract from the learning of another, as if there were to be a limited quantity to be divided into exclusive holdings... . That which one man gains by discovery is a gain to other men. And these multiple gains become invested capital... .

–John Wesley Powell, 1886

ABSTRACT

The restructuring of state education systems in many OECD countries during the last two decades has involved a significant shift away from an emphasis on *administration* and *policy* to an emphasis on *management*. The "new managerialism" has drawn theoretically, on the one hand, on the model of corporate managerialism and private sector management styles, and, on public choice theory and new institutional economics (NIE), most notably, agency theory and transaction cost analysis, on the other. A specific constellation of these theories is sometimes called "New Public Management," which has been very influential in the United Kingdom, Australia, Canada and New Zealand. These theories and models have been used both as the legitimation for policies that redesigning state educational bureaucracies, educational institutions and even the public policy process. Most importantly, there has been a decentralization of management control away from the center to the individual institution through a "new contractualism" – often referred to as the "doctrine of self-management" – coupled with new accountability and competitive funding regimes. This shift has often been accompanied by a disaggregation of large state bureaucracies into autonomous agencies, a clarification of organizational objectives, and a separation between policy advice and policy implementation functions, together with a privatization of service and support functions through "contracting out". The "new managerialism" has also involved a shift from input controls to quantifiable output measures and performance targets, along with an emphasis on short term performance contracts, especially for CEOs and senior managers. In the interests of so-called "productive efficiency," the provision of educational services has been made contestable; and, in the interests of so-called allocative efficiency state education has been progressively marketized and privatized. In this paper I analyze the main underlying elements of this theoretical development that led to the establishment of the neoliberal university in the 1980s and 1990s before entertaining and reviewing claims that new public management is dead. At the end of the paper I focus on proposals for new forms of 'the public' in higher education as a means of promoting "radical openness" consonant with the development of Web 2.0 technologies and new eresearch infrastructures in the global knowledge economy.

INTRODUCTION

After Nietzsche, the philosophical critique of the Western university has developed along two interrelated lines: the first, pursued by Weber and continued by Heidegger, Jaspers, Lyotard and Bourdieu emphasized the dangers of economic interest vested in the university through the dominance of *technical reason*; the second, initiated by members of the Frankfurt School and developed differently by Foucault, traces the imprint and controlling influence of the state in the academy through the apparatus of *administrative reason*. With the rise of the "neoliberal university" these two forms of reason have come together in a new constellation. First, through a capitulation of the norms of liberal humanism and the Kantian ethical subject the university has embraced the main articles of faith underlying the revitalization of economic rationalism and introduced the principle of *homo economicus* into university governance. Second, through the imposition of structural adjustments policies of the IMF based on the "Washington consensus" universities in the developing world during the 1980s were forced to privatize universities with devastating impacts.

Neoliberal universities, with little philosophical self-reflection, have been put in the service of the "new global economy" under conditions of *knowledge capitalism* that has had several effects.[1] First, it has diminished the public status of the university. In the era of sovereign debt crisis the search for alternative funding patterns have led to national strategies for encouraging fee-paying students on the basis of human capital theory, leading to excessive student debt and a consequent privatization of higher education. Second, it has buttressed domestic fee-paying students with an internationalization of higher education and the global competition for international students with the growth of multiple campuses and off-shore profit centers. Both these features led directly to the encouragement of all forms of capitalization of the self and a kind of new educational prudentialism (Peters, 2005). Third, it has focused on issues of intellectual capital and the ownership of the means of knowledge production with the development and expansion of research parks, private-public partnerships in science production, and an emphasis on the commercialization of research and online teaching initiatives. Fourth, it has led to the huge growth of administration *vis a vis* the teaching and research faculty, to an increasing bureaucratization of the university and to the emergence of a new class of "knowledge managers," – an administrative cadre— whose job is monitor and measure academic performance and to maximize returns from research.

Most of these developments leading to the neoliberal university and its recent variants—the "entrepreneurial university," the "enterprise university," the "innovation university"—spring from the application of neoliberal economics to higher education based on a series of reforms carried out in the 1980s and 1990s. In particular, the reforms often collectively referred to as "new managerialism" or "new public management," often applied to the reform of the public sector as a whole, have sprung from public choice theory and new institutional economics leading to a fundamental reframing of the university what Bill Readings has called "the university of excellence." The vice-chancellor, deans and heads of department have increasingly become "knowledge managers" in a knowledge corporation charged with running the university through a strategic planning process in accordance with targets, new incentive structures, and policy directives at the expense of traditional collegial and democratic governance. Governing councils have become corporate boards further sidelining academic forums. There is a new emphasis on executive-directed systems for internal university consultation and communication, from internal market research to vice-chancellors' advisory groups with the consequent decline of collegiality forums and faculty input into key governance decisions. The rise of new property structures concerning international education, intellectual property, relations with industry, and work-based training have thickened the relationship to industry without any compensating collegial structures. Research management is increasingly subject to the new discipline of performance system assessment as institutions gear up to deliver research outputs and competing for funding within increasingly sophisticated national funding output-driven performance systems. This has led to a diminishment of the role of peer input into decisions about research and the prioritization of research in terms of quantity of research income rather than in terms of numbers of publications produced or in terms of quality of scholarship (Marginson, 1999).

THEORETICAL ELEMENTS OF THE 'NEW MANAGERIALISM'

1. Public Choice Theory

Public choice theory applies the methods of economics to the study of political and administrative behavior. It originated with Gordon Tullock (editor of *Public Choice*) and James Buchanan, formerly of Virginia Polytechnic Institute and State University and now located at George Mason University at Virginia. The essence of public choice theory has been summed up by Buchanan (1980: 19–27) who identifies its two elements as the "catallactics" approach to economics (or "catallaxy" as Hayek terms it) and the classical *homo economicus* postulate concerning individual behavior normally interpreted in terms of three attributes: rationality, individuality and self-interest. Individuals are conceived as "rational utility-maximizers." "Catallactics" is the study of institutions of exchange which Buchanan deems the proper object of research and inquiry in economics. It allegedly rests on the principle of 'spontaneous order' most thoroughly developed in the work of Hayek who argues that unhampered markets, without government control or intervention, demonstrate a tendency to equilibrium. In Hayek's thought the spontaneous order conception applies to physical systems (for example, crystals and galaxies) as much as to social and cultural life (for example, the growth of language; the development of law and the emergence of social norms). We can distinguish three elements of the idea of spontaneous social order in Hayek's work:

- The invisible hand thesis that social institutions arise as a result of human action but not from human design;
- The thesis of the primacy of tacit or practical knowledge – a thesis which maintains that knowledge of the social world is embodied in practices and skills and only secondarily in theories;
- The thesis of the natural selection of competitive traditions in which 'traditions' are "understood to refer to complexes of practices and rules of action and perception and the claim is that there is a continuous evolutionary filtering of these traditions" (Gray, 1984, 33–34).

It is ultimately on the basis of this argument, originating in a critique of Cartesian rationalism that Hayek (distinct from Buchanan) claims that we must give up the modern ideal of an interventionist public policy and replace it with an ideal of cultivating general conditions within which benefits might be expected to emerge.

The main innovation of Buchanan and the public choice school is to apply this notion of spontaneous order conception beyond simple exchange (two commodities/two persons) to complex exchange and finally to *all processes of voluntary agreement* among persons. Buchanan (1986: 20) writes: "By a more or less natural extension of the catallactic approach, economists can look on politics and on political action in terms of the exchange paradigm." It is important to realize that this is the case so long as collective action is modeled with individual decision-makers as the basic units. The result of this conception is to confine politics to the realm of non-voluntary relationships among persons – that is, those relationships involving power or coercion. Normative implications are derived from public choice theory and carry with them an approach to institutional reform. To the extent that voluntary exchange is valued positively while coercion is valued negatively, public choice theorists favor market-like arrangements and/or the decentralization of political authority. The constitutional perspective is said to emerge naturally from the politics-as-exchange paradigm: "To improve politics it is necessary to improve or reform the rules, the framework within which the game is played ... A game is described by its rules, and a better game is produced only by changing the rules" (Buchanan, 1986: 22).

Buchanan (1986), following Wicksell (the Swedish economist and claimed precursor of public choice theory) states that if reform in economic policy is desired then we should look to the rules through which economic policy decisions get made, that is, look to the constitution itself. This conception has revolutionized "public choice" and provided a strong rationale and approach to the reform of the public sector. The second element of public choice theory is the behavioral postulate known as *homo economicus*, that is the modern "rediscovery" of the main tenet of classical liberal economics, that people should be treated as "rational utility-maximizers" in all of their behavior. In other words, individuals are modeled as seeking to further their own interests (defined in terms of measured net wealth positions) in politics as in other aspects of their behavior.

2. New Institutional Economics

Managerialism is a new form of governance based on constitutional or rule-making activity. As Davis (1997: 228) suggests the "new institutional economics encouraged policy-makers to see public services not as production functions or firms, but as governance structures". Institutional economics abandons the traditional notion of a firm as being a production function to see it as a governance structure that reduces transaction costs and market competition favors the governance structure with the most efficient solutions of the problems of transaction costs. The notion of economic efficiency in institutional economics has successful shifted ethos and practice of *management* to a question of the culture and structure of *governance* based on the value of customizing the service or product.

Neoliberalism is the substantive discourse of governance that is potent precisely because of is its capacity to combine economics, the social, and politics on behalf of rational choice as a principle of legitimacy. Governance arrangements have been classified into simple purchase and sale arrangements, bilateral arrangements for more complex relationships as for example, with joint ventures, trilateral arrangements where third parties are involved in processes such as arbitration and vertically integration where the transaction costs are reduced by forming a firm. While the institutional analysis of the public sector (for example, selecting governance structures which minimize transaction costs) is fundamentally concerned with the same issues as in the private sector, the actual issues and concepts of the public sector are different from the private sector for whereas in the private sector firms may fail, the same cannot be allowed for government structures even under marketized conditions.

The new institutional economics embraces at least two different strands of thought: agency theory and transaction cost analysis. Agency theory focuses on the problem of how to get agents to do what their principals want through contracts. While managerialism did not necessarily imply a move to contracting in the public sector, but it laid all the necessary foundations. Transaction cost analysis is concerned with concepts and principles for analyzing and controlling transactions though, for example, transparency, goals specification, clear allocation of decision rights, incentives, contracts and the credibility of commitments. Transaction costs are seen as the economic equivalent of friction in physical systems and transaction cost analysis is concerned with an examination of the comparative costs of planning, adapting and monitoring task completion under alternative governance structures. As the context for business changed difficulties in transacting business ensued whereupon attempts were made at designing new governance systems that would minimize the costs of such transactions.

We can also distinguish the old collectivist notion of the social contract from a "new contractualism" that represents a neoliberal politicization of public management. No longer are citizens presumed to be members of a political community that it is the business of a particular form of governance to express. The old presumed shared political process of the social contract disappears in favor of a disaggregated and individualized relationship to governance. Although contract can be regarded as a source of legitimacy – on the basis of the social contract – the idea of contract as an instrument of government can also be invoked. While contract theory is commonly regarded as addressing questions of the *legitimacy* of government, it can be seen as the core of an autonomous *rationality* of government on three counts: first, it specifies the population to be governed as "autonomous" citizens; second, it identifies a rationality of government that depends on no external principles; third, it tells us that individuals are to be governed on the basis of the presumed social contract.

3. New Public Management

During the 1980s and '90s a particular form of managerialism referred as New Public Management (NPM) (Boston, 1996; Boston, et.al., 1996; Hood, 1990, 1991, 1992; Aucion, 1988, 1990a, 1990b; Peters, 1990) or simply as public management (Pollitt, 1990: 156) came to dominate policy agendas. Pollitt (1992: 11) notes that the managerial literature contains little reference to the welfare state or the characteristic modes of thought of its policymakers, administrators and service providers. He notes that social needs, professional standards, deprivation, community and equity have historically played little or no part in the development of managerialism and writes: "the transfer, during the last decade or two, of managerialism from private sector corporations to welfare-state services represents the injection of an ideological 'foreign body' into a sector previously characterized by quite different traditions of thought" (Pollitt, 1992: 11).

Private sector management theory – notably the work of Drucker – had an influence on new public management outside economic theory. There is an extensive literature on strategic management and management by objectives which predate the new institutional economics but which arrives at similar conclusions about clear goals and reporting relationships. The emphasis, for example, on contracting could emerge from business management theory or public administration theory as no more than a useful technique to introduce clarity, transparency and competition into organization. Some scholars argue that the notion of public management does not differ substantially from private management (e.g., Martin, 1994).

The key features of new public management as developed in New Zealand as perhaps the most comprehensive model have been identified by Boston et al (1996: 4–5) as comprising three separate aspects: the broad objectives; the administrative principles; and the specific policies. In specific policy terms, the model developed in the mid 1990s exhibit the following features:

1. A preference for retaining key governmental powers and responsibilities at the central government level with only limited devolution to sub-national government despite considerable rhetoric about devolution in the 1980s.

2. A strong emphasis on the use of incentives to enhance performance, at both the institutional and the individual level (e.g., short term employment contracts, performance-based remuneration systems, promotion systems, etc.).
3. An extensive use of explicit, generally written 'contracts' of various kinds, which specify the nature of performance required and the respective obligations of agents and principals (e.g. performance agreements between ministers and department CEs, purchase agreements between ministers and departments, and contracts between funders and purchasers and between purchasers and providers). In addition to the emphasis on *ex ante* performance specification, more exacting monitoring and reporting systems have been introduced.
4. The development of an integrated and relatively sophisticated strategic planning and performance management system throughout the public sector. Key elements include the specification by ministers of strategic result areas and key result areas and the integration of these into CEs' performance agreements and departmental purchase agreements.
5. The removal, wherever possible, of dual or multiple accountability relationships within the public sector, and the avoidance of joint central and local democratic control of public services.
6. The institutional separation of commercial and non-commercial functions; the separation of advisory, delivery, and regulatory functions; and the related separation of the roles of funder, purchaser, and provider.
7. The maximum decentralisation of production and management decision-making, especially with respect to the selection and purchase of inputs and the management of human resources.
8. The implementation of a financial management system based on accrual accounting and including capital charging, a distinction between the Crown's ownership and purchaser interests, a distinction between outcomes and outputs, an accrual-based appropriations system, and legislation requiring economic policies that are deemed to be 'fiscally responsible'.
9. Strong encouragement for, and extensive use of, competitive tendering and contracting out, but few mandatory requirements for market testing or competitive tendering.

HNPM has gained political acceptance in at least three different countries: Australia, New Zealand and the United Kingdom. He says all of these three variants of NPM share some general features. They include the switch in emphasis from policy formulation to management and institutional design; a shift from process controls to output controls; a move from integration to differentiation and from statism to subsidiarity. Hood (1990) then gives five possible explanations for the rise of NPM in the late 1980s: First, NPM could be simply interpreted as a "mood swing" or passing fad. Second, NPM could be interpreted as a "new-look form of Treasury control with a set of doctrines fastened upon the financial by central controlling agencies to destroy the administrative bases of the public welfare lobby and to increase their own power *vis-a-vis* the professionalised line departments" (Hood, 1990: 206). Third, "parts of NPM could be seen as reflecting a new political campaign technology – the shift to public policy based on intensive opinion polling which is part of the new machine politics style" (Hood, 1990: 206). Fourth, NPM could reflect a "new client politics," the advent of a new easily mobilizable coalition whose collective self-interest drives a policy boom. This is sometimes referred to as the development of the new elite aiming at increasing their own powers of patronage and consisting of management consultants, financial intermediaries, insurance companies, and other groups that have a clear interest in privatization and contracting out. It is these people who give policy advice to government on what the rationality of government should be. Fifth, NPM could be interpreted as an administrative reflection of that broader set of social changes triggered by "post industrialism" or "post Fordism". Of the five possible explanations of the rise of NPM, the fifth is, according to Hood (1990: 207), this is the most complete.

Hood (1990: 214) considers that the NPM is not sufficiently theorized and concludes with a discussion about four possible areas of concern. The first concerns the change in public service ethics, loyalty to the service as a whole and resilience to political crisis: political accountability involves much more than achieving 'one line' results. The second concerns the problem of how to reconcile the Taylorist and 'new institutional economics' wings of NPM. Public choice has an inherently decentralist, consumer oriented bias, whereas the new Taylorism is about manipulation from above or from a controlling authority. The third concern is about the limits of the NPM revolution. There seems to be no end to the individualizing and atomization process. Hood refers to the possibility of selling government administrative positions so that the purchaser could then invest in the successful discharge of their duties. The fourth concern is the problem of exactly what kind of public service the NPM revolution is aiming to produce. Should the really high salaries go to the public sector or to the so-called private "wealth producing" sector? In the latter case, how then could the public sector attract the necessary talent? – or would it be then structured to produce the very mediocre performance that it was so criticized for in the past?

Pollitt (1990:25) draws attention to a recently emerging analysis that sets limits on the practical usefulness that managers can derive form any general theory of management. This failure is attributed to the idea that managerial skills differ considerably from other sorts of expertise in their limited standardization across industries, their susceptibility to change, their specificity to situations rather than problems and their diffuse, varied knowledge base. Effective management will require more than mere knowledge of management theory. This suggests that to the extent that we see the same model of management spread across all situations in the pubic sector, it will be appropriate to ask how realistic this is in terms of the very different requirements between the various public areas.

"NEW PUBLIC MANAGEMENT IS DEAD"

New public management is a management philosophy used governments to modernize and restructure the public sector based on the hypothesis that a more market orientation in the public sector will lead to greater cost-efficiency for governments, without negative side effects. Often the neoliberal restructuring reforms across the public sector with an emphasis on public health and the universities as two of the largest government portfolios focused on introducing competition in to the public sector through consumer-driven systems (citizens as shareholders), with strong attention to better management of the public budgetary process and a new accent on leadership.

By the end of 1990s commentators were heralding the end of public choice and new public management with a resurgence of institutional theories based on March and Olsen's (1984) famous paper. B. Guy Peters (2000) writes:

The past decade and a half have seen a major reassertion of institutional theories in the social sciences, and especially in political science. The March and Olsen (1984) article in the APSR was the beginning of the revolution against the methodological individualism of both behavioralism and rational choice approaches. Following from that and their subsequent publications (1989; 1994; Brunsson and Olsen, 1993; Olsen and Peters, 1996) there has been a proliferation of institutional theories and applications of those theories. Similarly, in economics (North, 1990; Alston, Eggerston and North, 1996; Khalil, 1995) and in sociology (DiMaggio and Powell, 1991; Scott, 1995; Zucker, 1987) there has been a birth (or more appropriately a resurrection) of institutional approaches to the basic questions in these disciplines.

A number of critics proclaim that NPM is "dead" and argue that the cutting edge of change has moved on to digital era governance (DEG) focusing on reintegrating concerns into government control, holistic (or joined-up) government and digitalization. DEG draws on principles of open government and utilizes the Web and digital storage to focus on transparency and better communication within government. For instance, Dunleavy and Margetts (2006) argue that NPM has stalled or been reversed because its complexity has reduced the capacity of citizens and public stakeholders to participate in the solution of social problems. They claim that next wave of technology-centered change is shifting toward "digital-era governance" (DEG), which involves reintegrating functions into the governmental sphere, adopting holistic and needs-oriented structures, and progressing digitalization of administrative processes.

Others associated with Public Value theory have re-asserted a focus on citizenship, networked governance and the role of public agencies in working with citizens to *co-create public value*, generate democratic authorization, and foster legitimacy and trust. They stress that the domains within which public managers are working as complex adaptive systems with characteristics that are qualitatively different from simple market forms, or private sector business principles (Moore, 1995; Cole & Parston, 2006; Cresswell et al. 2006).

In 2001 the European Commission wrote a white paper on governance entitled *European Governance* which begins with the following statement[2]:

Democratic institutions and the representatives of the people, at both national and European levels, can and must try to connect Europe with its citizens. This is the starting condition for more effective and relevant policies.

And continues

> The White Paper proposes opening up the policy-making process to get more people and organisations involved in shaping and delivering EU policy. It promotes greater openness, accountability and responsibility for all those involved.

The white paper proposes a change to "better involvement and openness" based on online information in the preparation of policy, more systematic dialogue with all constituencies, greater flexibility to accommodate local diversity, and the encouragement of partnership arrangements. The white paper also promotes "better policies, regulation and delivery," "global governance" and "refocused institutions."

RADICAL OPENNESS AND THE IDEA OF THE UNIVERSITY

Ron Barnett (2011: 3) is one author that has recognized the evolution of new institutional forms in higher education under conditions of neoliberal knowledge capitalism that tend toward the "hyper-modernisation" of the university. He writes:

> New institutional forms involving cross-institutional collaboration, a blurring of the public and the private, new learning modes (especially favouring e-learning and practice-based learning), forms of knowledge pursued for their "impact" on the knowledge economy, the rise of the "global" in higher education and the emergence of "nomadic" identities among academics: all these and more contribute to the "hyper-modernisation" of the university (cf. Lipovetsky, 2005).

He comments on the shift towards "performativity", the accent on so-called "useful knowledge" with direct applicability in society and "a slide away from 'liberal education' towards vocationalisation and the increasing influence of governments and inter-governmental agencies in encouraging these shifts" (pp. 4–5).

The 2008 global financial crisis was the consequence of the processes of both "financialization" and the hegemonic neoliberal ideology based on self-regulated and efficient markets. Neoclassical economics has played the role of a meta-ideology as it legitimized, mathematically and "scientifically," neoliberal ideology and deregulation (Bresser-Pereira, 2010). There is hope that from this crisis a new democratic capitalist system will emerge with tendencies toward a global and knowledge-economy based on an improved democracy that is more open, social and genuinely participative.

New forms of technological-enabled openness, especially emergent social media that utilizes social networking, blogs, wikis and user-created content and media, provide *new models of openness* for a conception of the intellectual commons based on peer production which is a radically decentralized, genuinely interactive, and collaborative form of knowledge sharing that can usefully serve as the basis of "knowledge cultures" (Peters & Besley, 2006; Peters & Roberts, 2011). The modern university was based on the principles of industrial broadcast mass media that was designed to reach large audience on a one-to-many logic. The open university is based on the new P2P architectures and technologies that are part of the ideology of Web 2.0 and given expression in ways that emphasize the ethic of participation ("participatory media"), collaboration and file-sharing characterizing the rise of social media (see Peters et al. 2011).

The modern university was an institution built on the principles of industrial media; the open university is an institution built upon the principles of social media providing the basis for a new social media model of the university that embraces the social democratic vision of the university and that it provides, first, the means to recover and enhance the historical mission of the university (Peters, 2007) and, second, a useful discourse to re-theorize the university in the twenty-first century, jettisoning its neoliberal managerialist ideology and returning to a fully socialized view of knowledge and knowledge-sharing that has its roots in Enlightenment thinking about science and its new practices in commons-based peer-production.

The *university model of open management* builds on both digital-era governance and the notion of public value and links effectively with moves to rebuild new forms of the public through principles of open governance. It is linked to the rejuvenation of open-source governance as a political theory that harnesses open source and open-content movements to democratic principles to promote collaborative and deliberative forms of open management characterized by the centrality of historic structures of peer review and peer governance. If the capacity to create knowledge – or what Italian autonomists call the 'general intellect' – is becoming the key productive force, arguably there is a need for a full-blown social form of knowledge management (Peters & Bulut, 2011; Peters & Reveley, 2012).

In the age of knowledge capitalism, we can expect governments in the West to further ease themselves out of the public provision of education as they begin in earnest to privatize the means of knowledge production and experiment with new ways of designing and promoting a permeable interface between knowledge businesses and public education at all levels. In the last two decades we have witnessed the effects of the Hayekian revolution in the economics of knowledge and information, we have experienced the attack on 'big government' and reductions of state provision, funding and regulation. In the age of knowledge capitalism the next great struggle after the "culture wars" and the "science wars" of the 1990s will be the "education wars," a struggle not only over the *meaning* and *value* of knowledge both internationally and locally, but also over the public means of knowledge production. As Michel Foucault (1991: 165) argued in the early 1980s in conversation with the Italian communist Duccio Trombadori:

We live in a social universe in which the formation, circulation, and utilization of knowledge presents a fundamental problem. If the accumulation of capital has been an essential feature of our society, the accumulation of knowledge has not been any less so. Now, the exercise, production, and accumulation of this knowledge cannot be dissociated from the mechanisms of power; complex relations exist which must be analysed.

The problem of the accumulation of knowledge – a new accumulation regime at the very heart of knowledge capitalism—is a complex layered system comprised on at least three components: the content layer; the code layer; and the infrastructure layer. Where content can be open and free, code and infrastructure is generally owned. This is the essence of "algorithmic knowledge capitalism" (Peters, 2011) and clearly evident in the development of a cybernetic informational capitalism and the recent emergence of the giant info-utilities like Google, Amazon.com and Microsoft.

The learned society provides a model that is neither state nor market that has a long history of a commitment to public knowledge and science based on peer review and governance as an essential characteristic of science and scholarship, along with replicability, testability and the cultivation of a critical attitude that is the essence of peer review. Learned societies also provide a useful set of norms upon which to generalize and establish the learning society as a generalized science model committed to the public good. In the digital age new Web 2.0 technologies and forms of social media provide new ways of enhancing and building upon the peer production of knowledge. The Internet has become the foundational cyberinfrastructure that facilitates scholarly communication and deep data-sharing, archiving and publishing affecting every stage of the scholarly production, transforming the historical concepts that historically comprised the legal and economic architecture that grew up around intellectual property rights and the emergence of the concept of the public in its modern sense. Mass digitization of books, electronic books and new forms of open journals systems have greatly expanded the availability of scholarly publication and scientific data changing both the logics of production and consumption (reception) of academic texts. New models of open science and open knowledge production based on principles of global public goods and an ethos of sharing and collaboration create new transnational academic communities in global knowledge ecologies that intersect in novel ways. Now is the time to experiment with and institute new university models of open management that recognize the vital role of the *public* university and its role in the production of knowledge and citizens for knowledge democracies.

NOTES

[1] On higher education and the forms of the knowledge economy, see Peters & Besley (2006), Peters (2007), Murphy, Peters & Marginson (2010), Marginson, Murphy & Peters (2010), Araya & Peters (2010), Peters (2010), Peters & Bulut (2011), Peters & Reveley (2012).

[2] See the governance website at http://europa.eu.int/comm/governance/index_en.htm.

REFERENCES

Araya, D. & M. A. Peters, (2010). (Eds.). *Education in the Creative Economy*. New York, Peter Lang.
Aucoin, P. (1988). 'Contraction, Managerialism and Decentralisation in Canadian Government'. *Governance: An International Journal of Policy and Administration, 1*(2), 144–161.

Aucoin, P. (1990a). 'Administrative Reform in Public Management: Paradigms, Principles, Paradoxes and Pendulums'. In: *Governance: An International Journal of Policy and Administration, 3*(2), 115–137.

Aucoin, P. (1990b). 'Comment: Assessing Managerial Reforms'. In: *Governance: An International Journal of Policy and Administration, 3*(2) 197–204.

Barley, S. & G. Kunda. (1992). 'Design and Devolution: Surges of Rational and Normative Ideologies of Control in Managerial Discourse'. *The Administrative Science Quarterly, 37, 3*.

Barnett, R. (2011). Being a university (foundations and futures of education). New York: Routledge.

Bell, D. (1976). *The Coming of the Post-Industrial Society: A Venture in Social Forecasting*. Basic Books. (1973 original edition).

Boston, J, J. Martin, J. Pollot, & P. Walsh. (1996). *Public Management: The New Zealand Model*. Melbourne: Oxford University Press.

Boston, J. (1996). 'Origins and destinations: New Zealand's model of public management and the international transfer of ideas', in Weller, P. & G. Davis. (Eds.) *New Ideas, Better Government*. NSW: Allen & Unwin: 107–131.

Boston, J., J. Martin, J. Pallot, & P. Walsh. (Eds.). (1991). *Reshaping The State: New Zealand's Bureaucratic Revolution*. Auckland: Oxford University Press.

Bresser-Pereira, L.C. (2010). 'The Global Financial Crisis and a New Capitalism?' Working Paper, 592, Levy Economic Institute.

Buchanan, J. & G. Tullock. (1962). *The Calculus of Consent: Logical Foundations of Constitutional Democracy*. Michigan: Ann Arbor Paperback.

Cole, M. & Parston, G. (2006). *Unlocking Public Value*, John Wiley & Sons.

Cresswell, A.M., Burke, G.B. & Pardo, T.A. (2006). *Advancing Return on Investment Analysis for Government: A Public Value Framework*, The Center for Technology in Government, University at Albany, State University of New York.

Davis, G. (1996). 'Making sense of difference? Public choice, politicians and bureacratic change in America and Australia', in Weller, P. & G. Davis. (Eds.) *New Ideas, Better Government*. NSW: Allen & Unwin: 305–317.

Davis, G. (1997). 'Implications, consequences and futures', in Davis, G. B. Sullivan & A. Yeatman (Eds.) *The New Contractualism?* Melbourne: Macmillan: 224–238.

Drucker, P. (1974). *Management*. London: Butterworth Heinemann.

Drucker, P. (1994). *Post Capitalist Society*. Oxford: Buttertworth Heinemann.

Dunleavy, P. & Helen Margetts, H. (2006). 'New Public Management is Dead: Long Live Digital Era Governance', *Journal of Public Administration Research and Theory, 16*(3), 467–94.

Enteman, W. (1993). *Managerialism: The Emergence of a New Ideology*. Wisconsin: The University of Wisconsin Press.

Foucault, M. (1991). Discipline and Punish: the birth of a prison. London: Penguin.

Handy, C. (1976). *Understanding Organizations*. Harmondsworth: Penguin.

Hindess, B. (1997). 'A society governed by contract?', in Davis, G. B. Sullivan & A. Yeatman (Eds.) *The New Contractualism?* Melbourne: Macmillan: 14–26.

Hogan, D. (1997). 'The social economy of parent choice and the contract state'. In, Weller, P. & G. Davis, (Eds.). *New Ideas, Better Government*. NSW: Allen & Unwin: 119–136.

Hood, C. (1990). 'De- Sir Humphreyfying the Westminster model of Bureaucracy: A New Style of Governance'? *Governance: An International Journal of Policy and Administration, 3*(2), 205–214.

Hood, C. (1991). 'A Public Management For All Seasons?'. *Public Administration, 69*(Spring), 3–19.

Hood, C. (1992). 'The new public management model and its conceptions of performance engineering'. In: *The Public Sector Challenge: Defining, Delivering and Reporting Performance*. New Zealand Society of Accountants Public Sector Convention. Plaza Hotel, Wellington: 35–50.

Kondo, D. (1990). *Crafting Selves: Power, Gender And Discourses Of Identity In A Japanese Workplace*. Chicago: The University of Chicago Press.

Lipovetsky, G. (2005). Hypermodern times. Cambridge: Polity Press.

March, J.G. & Olsen, J.P. (1984). The new institutionalism: Organizational factors in political life." *American Political Science Review*, 78, p. 734–49.

Marginson, S., Murphy, P. & Peters, M.A. (2010). Global Creation: Space, Mobility and Synchrony in the Age of the Knowledge Economy. New York, Peter Lang.

Martin, J. (1994). 'The Role of the State in Administration'. In: Sharp, Andrew (Ed). *Leap Into The Dark: The Changing Role of the State in New Zealand Since 1984*. Auckland, Auckland University Press: 41–67.

Moore, M. (1995). *Creating Public Value Strategic Management in Government*, Harvard University Press.

Murphy, P., Peters, M.A. & Marginson, S. (2010). *Imagination: Three Models of Imagination in the Age of the Knowledge Economy*. New York, Peter Lang.

Perrow, C. (1979). *Complex Organizations: A Critical Essay*. London: Scott Forseman and Co. (2nd Edition).

Peters, B.G. (2000). Institutional theory: Problems and prospects. *Institute for Advanced Studies*, 69, p. 1–28.

Peters, M.A. (2005). 'The New Prudentialism in Education: Actuarial rationality and the entrepreneurial self,' *Educational Theory*, 55(2), 123–137 (15).

Peters, M.A. (2007). *Knowledge Economy, Development and the Future of Higher Education*. Rotterdam, Sense Publishers.

Peters, M.A. (2010). Three Forms of Knowledge Economy: Learning, Creativity, Openness, *British Journal of Educational Studies*, 58(1), 67–88.

Peters, M.A. & Besley, Tina (A.C.) (2006). *Building Knowledge Cultures: Education and Development in the Age of Knowledge Capitalism*. Lanham, Boulder, NY, Oxford, Rowman & Littlefield.

Peters, M.A. & Reveley, J. (2012). Retrofitting Drucker: Knowledge work under cognitive capitalism. Unpublished article.

Peters, M.A. & Bulut, E. (2011). (Eds.). *Cognitive Capitalism, Education and the Question of Digital Labor*. New York: Peter Lang.

Peters, M.A. & Roberts, P. (2011). *The Virtues of Openness: Education, Science and Scholarship in a Digital Age*. Boulder, Paradigm Publishers.

Peters, M.A., Gietzen, G. & Ondercin, D. (2011). 'Knowledge Socialism: Intellectual Commons and Openness in the University.' In R. Barnett (Ed.), *The Future University*. London: Routledge, pp. 187–200.

Peters, M.A., Murphy, P. & Marginson, S. (2009). *Creativity and the Global Knowledge Economy*. New York, Peter Lang.

Pollitt, C. (1990). *Managerialism and the Public Services: The Anglo – American Experience*. Oxford: Basil Blackwell.

Powell, J., 1886. In: *Testimony Before the Joint Commission* (letter to W. B. Allison,February 26, 1886), 1082.

Pusser, B., Kempner, K., Marginson, S. & Ordorika, I. (2010). *Universities and the Public Sphere:*

Scott, G. (1997). 'The new institutional economics and reshaping the state in New Zealand'. In Davis, G. B. Sullivan & A. Yeatman (Eds.) *The New Contractualism*? Melbourne: Macmillan: 154–163.

Sullivan, B. (1997). Mapping Contract. In, Davis, G. B. Sullivan & A. Yeatman (Eds.) *The New Contractualism*? Melbourne: Macmillan: 1–13.

Taylor, F. W. (1911). *Principles of Scientific Management*. New York: Harper.

LEARNED SOCIETIES, PUBLIC GOOD SCIENCE AND OPENNESS IN THE DIGITAL AGE

How few secrets have there been that have been long conceal'd from the whole World by their Authors? ... There is no question at all, but all, or the greatest part [of them] will soon flow into this *public Treasure.*

–Thomas Sprat, *History the Royal Society,* 1667, p. 74.

He who receives an idea from me, receives instruction himself without lessening mine; as he who lights his taper at mine, receives light without lessening mine.

–Thomas Jefferson, 1813

The learning of one man does not subtract from the learning of another, as if there were to be a limited quantity to be divided into exclusive holdings... . That which one man gains by discovery is a gain to other men. And these multiple gains become invested capital... .

–John Wesley Powell, 1886

SECTION I: THE PAST

INTRODUCTION: THE RISE OF LEARNED SOCIETIES AND THE PUBLIC NATURE OF SCIENCE

This paper comprises two sections, an historical oriented understanding of scientific societies and a future orientation based on new opportunities afforded societies in a digital age. The first part of the paper charts the rise of scientific learned societies, with a focus on the Royal Society based on the inspiration of Francis Bacon, and their links to the public nature of science with the aim of demonstrating the role and contribution of scientific learned societies to a contemporary understanding of science as a global public good. The second part of the paper, adopting a future perspective, examines 'learning societies', knowledge creation and journals systems, and the changing nature of scholarship in a digital age with new opportunities for peer-based commons production in the global science knowledge economy.

According to The Scholarly Societies Project[1] there are some 4,157 learned societies with 3,832 associated websites.[2] The oldest learned societies, some thirty of them, were established in the period 1323–1599 overwhelmingly in Italy (19 of 30), but also in France, England, Ireland, Scotland and Spain. The oldest academy in Europe was established in 1323 by seven wealthy men, "les sept Troubadours", who brought together poets writing in the langue d'Oc, to found *Compagnie du Gai Sçavoir*. Under Louis XIV, it became *Académie des Jeux Floraux* (*Academy of Floral Games*). In the period 1600 to 1699 a further 43 societies were established again predominantly in Europe (mostly Italy) with some societies being founded in Germany. During this period the Royal Society of London was established (1660) and the establishment of national science academies followed soon after.

James E. McClelland (2002) remarks:

> The organizational and institutional character of eighteenth-century learned societies developed from Renaissance antecedents and the humanist movement. By the fifteenth century, Renaissance humanism began to take on significant organizational and institutional dimensions, and hundreds of literary and fine arts societies sprang up outside the universities, wherever educated people gathered. Ficino's Accademia Platonica, founded in Florence in 1442, is sometimes pointed to as the first of this new type of organization, although Michele Maylender signals the Accademia Aldina (1495), associated with the Aldine press, as the first formal "Renaissance" academy.

The Renaissance academies 'changed [the] conditions for the organization of learning in the early modern period' developing a civil and public function that developed charters and were official corporate bodies receiving financial support from the state. Unlike the universities they had no institutional goals and did no teaching. Learned societies in the eighteenth century were complimentary to universities: the former were responsible for creating knowledge while the later transmitted it. McClelland notes:

> The number of official learned societies grew exponentially after 1700 as part of a Europe-wide institutional movement. Among scientific societies, for example, the first half of the century witnessed the creation of the leading national institutions: London (1662), Paris (1666), Berlin (1700), Saint Petersburg (1724), Stockholm (1739), and Copenhagen (1742). Major provincial and regional societies arose at this time in Montpellier (1706), Bordeaux (1712), Bologna (1714), Lyons (1724), Dijon (1725, 1740), and Uppsala (1728). The period following 1750 saw the appearance of societies in lesser European states and provinces...

In a growing and maturing relationship between state and institution learned societies offered expertise and the state offered legal protection and financial support. Societies took different forms: fine arts and language academies and scientific societies. Both became important for fostering ideas and experiment science through publication of proceedings of members' work that was presented. Learned society journals in the natural sciences, while only about a quarter of all journals in the field, accounted for most of the important and original science. What is more, the societies came to formalize interorganizational links with other societies across national boundaries beginning in the mid-eighteenth century extending the idea of public institutions into a network of scientific agencies. Many of the national societies formulated their research goals, undertook systematic research and sponsored expeditions. These societies were also responsible for setting up laboratories and organizing and sponsoring collections and libraries.

Martha Ornstein's (1963/1928) Seminal work entitled *Rôle of Scientific Societies in the Seventeenth Century* was originally a doctoral dissertation completed in 1913. She explains scientific advance in the seventeenth century first through the role of individual scientists (e.g., Galileo, Bacon, Descartes) (Part 1) and then through learned societies and their journals (part 2) focusing on the Italian scientific societies before turning to the Royal Society, the Academie des Sciences, German scientific societies, and the journals. Finally, she entertains the relationship between learned societies and the universities. She begins her account by analyzing the significance of Rosenberger's assertion that 'the seventeenth century introduced experiment into science' and all that it implied: its emphasis on measurement and exact observation, the production of instruments, and the creation of laboratories as places to conduct such experiments. Before the seventeenth century there were no such places as laboratories except for chemistry which grew out of alchemy with its apothecaries, furnaces and glass containers. While her arguments rests on the importance of experiment and observation that further demanded precise measurement and 'demonstrable facts', introducing a dynamism into science, Ornstein does not place enough significance on the relationship between alchemy and chemistry in the birth of experimental science.

The rise of learned societies and national academies in the late seventeenth and eighteenth centuries was the main form for the pursuit of cultural and scientific activities. These societies became quickly associated with the norms of open and free inquiry and tended to make public esoteric knowledge that had previously been secret in the so-called secret societies that developed during the Renaissance. Francis bacon famously railed against the secrets of alchemy and criticized Boyle for being too close to secret orders. William Eamon (1985) suggests that the essential feature of modern science is its public nature that is expressed in terms of the free sharing and exchange of knowledge and the spirit of collaborative inquiry determine by consensus arrived at through peer review, replication of experiment, and unbiased criticism by disinterested investigators. The consensus and it objectivity rests upon the free and open communication of the results of research that exemplifies the fundamental ethos and principle of open discourse and open disclosure. In this context secrecy 'is universally regarded as a dangerous enemy of the advancement of science. One might assume that a rule so central to modern science should have been a part of the tradition from its origins in antiquity. Instead, it developed relatively recently, at least in historical terms' (p. 321) Eamon explains that

> Only in the sixteenth and seventeenth centuries, with the emergence of new technology, new institutions for the promotion of scientific activity, and institutional mechanisms to protect the interests of discoverers, did the conception of science as "public knowledge" take form. These developments resulted in changes in the mechanisms for the dissemination of scientific

knowledge, and also in a transformation of the ethics governing the relationship between science and its public (p. 321).

Eamon links the 'opening up' of the closed world of medieval science based on secret societies and self-governing autonomous nature of universities that existed in self-imposed isolation to the printing press which revolutionized scientific communication and transformed the exchange, organization and governance of knowledge. Secret societies and sacred knowledge traditions as expressed by the pseudo-Aristotelian *Kitab Sirr al-Asrar* ("The Book of the Secret of Secrets"), known to Europeans as the *Secretum secretorum*—one of the most popular books in the Middle Ages—'professed to reveal the deepest, esoteric wisdom of Aristotle, but also promulgated the view that, with the aid of this secret knowledge, limitless things are possible in the material world' (p. 324). One biographer suggests that upon reading the work Roger Bacon turned from his interest in philosophy and theology to experimental science, making his own edition of the work. Secrecy was an ethical obligation to protect the 'divine science' from public view to be shared with those initiated into the responsibilities of a society and sworn to secrecy.[3] This was also the age when the development of the right to intellectual property emerged as a significant element in the move from 'secrets of nature' to public knowledge:

> The concept of the right of intellectual property, guaranteed through patents and copyrights, emerged in response to a growing awareness that scientific knowledge could be put to practical use, and that as long as new discoveries were kept secret, the advance of knowledge, and hence profit, would be retarded (Eamon, 1985: 329).

The concept and practice of the patent grew rapidly in the sixteenth century to ensure inventors their claim to the priority of their discovery and copyright was soon also expanded to the realm of pure ideas.

By the end of the eighteenth century learned societies proliferated across the disciplines. They had become the major vehicles for the creation of new scientific knowledge closely related to developments of journal systems and the dissemination of knowledge but also, perhaps more crucially, a commitment to the public nature science and knowledge. They became responsible for taking on civic functions of issuing standards in architecture, of popularizing standard works through dictionaries, encyclopedias and other reference works. They were institutions that stood for principles of public science and knowledge committed to the public good and structured and governed through peer mechanisms.

EXPERIMENTAL SCIENCE IN THE AGE OF MAGIC

Roy Porter, Katharine Park, Lorraine Daston (2006) approach 'the age of the new' through an examination of library classification systems that traced disciplinary formations and the birth of the sciences which from the Latin *scientia* simply meant any rigorous body of knowledge that could be demonstrated through syllogistic demonstrations of first premises. Natural philosophy, sometimes also *scientia naturalis,* concerned itself with change in the material world as well as metaphysical questions of time and space, seeking universal causes. Alchemy was different from the other subject—astronomy – that also preexisted the seventeenth century developing a century earlier with links going back beyond the discovery of the Copernican universe.

There is now little doubt that the beginnings of experimental science has its roots in the history of secret societies based on esoteric religion, alchemy and magic with a self-conscious lineage going back into the ancient world of Zarathrustra, the Persian priest, Pythagoras, and forms of neo-Platonism. Secret societies developing in the Renaissance drew on the work of Hermes Trimegistus, forms of Gnosticism (*gnosis* meaning 'knowledge'), the Cathars, the Knights Templar, forms of esoteric Judaism such as Cabalism and even aspects of the history of Shi'ite Islam. Both astrology and alchemy had been a mixture of the scientific and the spiritual and had been long practiced well before the Hermetic philosophers followed the works of Marsilio Ficino (1433–99) including the *Corpus Mermeticum. This was the age of the Florentine Giovanni Pico della Mirandola* (1463–94), Francesco Giogi (1466–1540)—both influence by Pico— Cornelius Agrippa (1486–1535), Paracelsus (1493–1541), John Dee (1527–1608), Giorando Bruno (1548–1600) and Francis bacon (1561–1626), many of whom were scholars, monks, physicians or surgeons, and philosophers. Some, in addition, had historical links to the Rosicrucians and Freemasonry and sought to make safe the secrets from the Roman Catholic Church.[4]

It is in this context in early modern England in the seventeenth century that the secrets of alchemy were first made public. Lauran Kassall (2001) records the books on alchemy underwent rapid growth during the sixty years after 1600 with '198 volumes containing 320 alchemical titles had been printed in English' (p. 66). Kassall (2011) explains how Boyle and Newton had 'rehabilitating alchemy, replacing her mystical green robes with the white coat of science' and going on to write:

> In the late seventeenth century laboratory alchemy reached new heights of sophistication, prompted by, for instance, Johann van Helmont's combination of Geberian corpuscularianism and Paracelsian vitalism. Alchemy became a subject identified with experimental philosophy. Weight superseded quality as a measure of chymical processes; salt began to be investigated as the secret of creation; and alchemical conventions of witnessing informed the notions of testimony established in the early Royal Society (p. 62).

The leaders of the emerging natural sciences assumed a strong and unbroken identity between knowing and being and thus a concept of divine knowledge that served as the ideal of science. Scientific method if it was anything solid, was sourced in a new experimental empiricism and objective observation on the one hand and the application of mathematics on the other, that was meant to purge science of all subjective contaminations. Rationality and reliability was ultimately sourced in God and the resulting knowledge was deemed to be indubitable and true. John Henry (2002) in his *The Scientific Revolution and the Origins of Modern Science* suggests that

> The natural philosophy of the Middle Ages, which had tended to remain aloof from mathematic and more pragmatic or experimental arts and sciences, became amalgamated with these other approaches to the analysis of nature, to give rise to something much closer to our notion of science (p. 5)

In "Magic and the Origins of Modern Science" Henry (1999) explains:

> Without the tradition of European magic, science and scientific medicine could hardly have developed as successfully as they have. The historical evidence for the crucial role of magic in the origins of modern science is totally compelling. But to recognise this evidence we have to become historically aware that magic was once rather different from what it has become. Barely understood today, natural magic was, for the first 700 years of this millennium, the predominant kind of magic. It was based upon the assumption that God had created the world as a continuous "Great Chain of Being", and that all the individual elements in creation were not only linked to one another through this unbroken chain, but that there were correspondences by which a creature in one part of the chain might resonate with, or somehow correspond to, a creature in another part of the chain. Underlying all this was a pervasive belief in purpose. God, or Nature, did nothing in vain, so there must be a reason for everything.

In the historiography of modern science whether one embraces the concept of scientific revolution with Thomas Kuhn or a notion of continuism, it is clear that the 'take off' of science was contemporaneous with its institutionalization and with the growth scientific learned societies and their commitment to public good science.

FRANCIS BACON'S 'EXPERIMENTALL LEARNING' AND THE RISE OF THE ROYAL SOCIETY

John Henry (2002) concedes that Francis Bacon "made no new discoveries, developed no technical innovations, uncovered no previously hidden laws of nature" yet nevertheless he is convinced of Bacon's importance as "a philosopher of science—perhaps the first one who really mattered". Before Bacon, he argues, "there was no such thing as science in our modern sense of the word" He points to three key factors comprising Bacon's importance: an insistence on experimental method rather than armchair speculation; the notion that a new knowledge of nature should be turned to the practical benefit of mankind; and the championing of inductive over deductive logic. "In a very real sense," he concludes," Bacon invented modern science."

Bacon invented modern science in another sense as well. As a civil servant Bacon believed in a useful science that can and should be pursued in the public interest under the aegis of the state, a vision he explains in the description of Solomon's House in Bacon's fable *New Atlantis*. He was the first to put forward a coherent view on how to use the power of modern science for the benefit of mankind aiming at power over nature in order to improve the human condition. His awareness of the need for systematic experimental scientific methodology together with his vision on the aims of public good science and an understanding of the essentials for developing a close relationship between scientific institutions and the state, initiated an ideology of science as a linear, progressive and cumulative basis for human progress that became the driving force of the Baconian program during the Enlightenment.

Yet as William Lynch argues historians of science have challenged the view that scientific practice follow or adhere to the norms and procedures of methodologies and now tend to see method as *post hoc* rationalization of culturally embedded scientific practice. By contrast, reference to a shared methodology or philosophy of science is now seen as part of the collective appeal to satisfy a pragmatic need to legitimate new approaches to science. This was surely the case with the Royal Society.

The frontispiece by Wenceslaus Hollar, after John Evelyn 1667, to *The History of the Royal-Society of London* (1667) by Thomas Sprat is a prime example of legitmation of a certain Baconian view of science. It shows three figures: William Brouncker, 2nd Viscount Brouncker, King Charles II, and Francis Bacon, Viscount St Alban. The bust of Charles II, the Society's first patron is being crowned by a symbolical figure representing Fame. Viscount Brouncker, the first president (left) points to the inscription. Francis Bacon, (Viscount St. Alban), is located to the right. At Bacon's feet is the legend 'Artium Instaurator', reminding us of his *Instauratio Magma.*

Figure 1. Frontispiece of Thomas Sprat's History of the Royal-Society, *engraved by Wenceslaus Hellar in 1667. Source: National Portrait Gallery (UK).[5]*

As Patricia Fara (2003) remarks:

> Sprat's *History of the Royal-Society* appeared in 1667, only five years after the fledgling Society was granted its Royal Charter and appointed its first President. Since there had not been much time for progress, Sprat concentrated on making grandiose claims for the future. To reinforce his message of Baconian improvement, Sprat included this engraving, even though it was too big to fit in his book without folding. Originally in a slightly different version, it had probably been designed as a broadsheet in the campaign to advertise the Royal Society and 'to devise all wayes to revive Lord Bacons lustre.'

Fara's analysis of the engraving is worth quoting in full for it serves to indicate the contextual and rhetorical elements that figured strongly in the legitimation of the Society:

> In this allegorical picture, Charles II is being crowned with a laurel wreath by the winged Goddess of Fame, immediately identifiable by her trumpet. Above his head hangs the Society's coat of arms, with its motto *Nullius in verba* – take nothing on authority – and behind the President's back lies the Society's large ornate mace, made of silver and a gift from the King. Diplomatically, Charles has been given the most prominent position in the hope of securing further royal patronage, preferably in the form of financial support (his generosity was mainly restricted to supplying his Society with venison for anniversary meetings). To demonstrate the Fellows' Baconian faith in experiment, the elegant arches are adorned with measuring instruments and in the background lie two of the Royal Society's crowning achievements, a giant telescope and the airpump designed by the aristocratic chemist, Robert Boyle.

> Elevated on his pillar, Charles is flanked by two figureheads who are identified but not named by the Latin words at their feet – the President and the Instaurator of the Arts (a more colloquial but anachronistic translation might be Promoter of Practical Science). This is a symbolic President: nominated by the King and here representing the Fellows of the Royal Society, his personal identity is irrelevant. He is timelessly draped in semi-classical attire, but the Society's ideological leader, Francis Bacon, is dressed in his old-fashioned Lord Chancellor's robes in the hope of attracting young lawyers to join the Society. The living President's gesture emphasizes the royal patron's importance, whereas Bacon is a guide from the past who indicates that instruments are the true source of knowledge.

Julie Robinson (2005) Positively reviews E.O. Wilson's claim that Bacon was the 'grand architect of the Enlightenment' which he bases on the fact that Bacon was intent on the organization of the disciplines and advocated a method that could serve and also help unify all branches of learning. Robinson emphasizes that Bacon insisted on the remaking of traditional knowledge so that it weaknesses were discovered and overcome by induction and experiment. William Lynch (2005) considers the way in which members of the Royal Society pursued his methodological prescription engendering a methodological unity within diversity through a focus on 'things in themselves' which could be interpreted in three distinct but overlapping ways: knowledge in the form of simple observation of fact; experimental construction of material effects; and, "theoretical realism" – "the belief that nature contain primal powers or forms that the natural philosopher could learn to assemble or 'alphabetize'in order to generate or 'spell' nature's complex physical processes" (Robinson, 2005:8). In other words, "Bacon's philosophy of science incorporated three different conceptions of knowledge: empiricism, constructivism and theoretical realism, corresponding to three different metaphors of "things in themselves" (Lynch, 2005: 202).

Alan Cook (1997) reviewing Edward Grant's (1996) *The Foundations of Modern Science in the Middle Ages* and Benedino Gemelli's (1996) *Aspetti dell'Atomismo classico nella Filosofia di Francis Bacone nel Seicento* suggests that the seeds of the scientific revolution were long in germinating. The Newtonian revolution that took place in the hundred years between 1650–1750 looks back metaphysical and theological issues of the Middle Ages. The philosophical basis of natural philosophy were explored in debates around classical sources that had been translated from Greek into Latin and supplemented by translations from the Arabic of commentaries on the Greek works along with Islamic original works. He continues:

Francis Bacon in the early 17th century had a very clear notion of the aims and possibilities of natural philosophy. Consequently many of the founders of the Royal Society looked back to him as their guide and inspiration, but his place in the actual development of science is ambiguous. He is probably best known today for advocating the inductive way to natural knowledge: collect as many facts of observation and experiment as possible, and infer general relations from them. His scheme was a sort of mechanization of discovery that was impractical in his day, but is akin to current ideas for using computers to collect and organize data and make inferences from them. Bacon himself seems to have realized that such a mechanical scheme must at least be supplemented by making observations specifically to answer questions that arose from speculative imagination. While he was greatly admired in his day, his method was also criticized, as by Sprat in *The History of the Royal Society of London*, who wrote of Bacon, 'His Rules were admirable: yet his History not so faithful, as might have been wish'd in many places, he seems rather to take all that comes, than to choose; and to heap, rather, than to register' (pp. 329–30). While no one ever made a discovery following Bacon's method, he was important in other ways: he discussed the four classes of failings that distort our knowledge of the natural world (idols of the tribe, of the cave, of the market place and of the theatre); he made sure that the results of natural knowledge should be consistent with religion; he championed ancient atomic theory; and he attacked 'the mysticism and magic of the Renaissance to develop a rational account of nature' (p. 333) even although some attitudes persisted.

In exploring the beginnings of an explanatory interest in science Stephen Turner (2008) enhances this understanding of Bacon's importance as providing a political vision of science that in essence formulated and helped to institutionalize public good science:

> The *fons et origo* of this discussion is Francis Bacon's vision of a political order in which the class of scientists is given power by an enlightened ruler in his House of Solomon in "The New Atlantis" ([1627]1882 v.5: 347–413). This vision had a practical effect on the attempts by the Royal Society in London to distinguished itself by its methodological practices and internal governance as a type of political body in relation to the crown (Sprat [1667]1958: 321–438; Lynch 2001: 177–96; Shapin 1994), and to do the same with parallel institutions elsewhere in Europe (Hahn 1971: 1–34; Gillispie 2004). The Victorians made sure that Bacon would be best known for his ideas about induction as a method (cf. Peltonen 1996: 321–24) and, as his major German expositor put it, "how his whole nature was, in every way, instinctively opposed to verbal discussions" (Fischer 1857: 307). But Bacon's extensive body of writings included not only writings on method, but also on "counsellors" to the crown, or experts, on the merits of republics, on the nature of political authority, on the proper internal organization of science, on funding and authority over science, and on collective research.

Science is the engine of progress, a picture that emerges more clearly in its recognizable modern form in Condorcet's "Fragment on Bacon's *New Atlantis*" (1793) with attention paid to the autonomy of science and freedom from political control, its internal governance and the forms of association. For Condorcet, drawing on Bacon's vision, the preferred method for extending the benefits of science was through education which was useful and enabled them to think for themselves. Yet as Turner recognizes education was considered politically ambiguous in that it required the exercise of state power and submission to the authority of science and reason thus amounting to expert rule with democratic consent. (Turner, 2008: 2). Later in the hands of saint-Simon and Comte science comes to replace politics altogether determined 'capacities' within the natural order and hierarchy of society as revealed by science. The tension between democratic free discussion and science driven by experts was not resolved by John Stuart Mill who was torn between his faith in liberty on the one hand and his methodological view that knowledge by induction led to proven results on the other.

SCIENCE AS A GLOBAL PUBLIC GOOD

Dana Dalrymple (2003) states: 'Scientific knowledge in its pure form is a classic public good.' Its benefits are many from technical advances that power innovation and economic growth to science-based policy advice. The concept of public good goes back at least to Adam Smith (1776) in maintaining public institutions and public works, and the argument for regarding science as a public good goes back explicitly to Bacon. Dalrymple (2003) acknowledges that it was William Whewell in 1840 who proposed the term 'scientist' instead of natural philosopher. She goes on to record:

> Bacon, among his other insights, was perhaps the first to record his views on the wider nature of knowledge when he wrote: "For the benefits of discoveries may extend to the whole human race" and "for virtually all time" (Bacon, 1620/2000, p. 99). He clearly saw the benefits of attempting to reach beyond national boundaries, as was evident in his treatment of three levels of ambition, the third of which was put in these terms:[6] "But if a man endeavor to establish and extend the power and dominion of the human race itself over the universe, his ambition ... is without a doubt both a more wholesome thing and more noble than the other two" (Henry 2002, p. 16).

Theories of public good develop in the late 19th century and in economics the term is generally traced back to Paul Samuelson (1954) in 'The Pure Theory of Public Expenditure' who formalizes the concept which he calls 'collective consumption goods' as goods that are essentially non-rival and non-excludable such that anyone can consume as much as desired without reducing the amount available for others. Thus, multiple individuals can consume the same good without diminishing its value (non-rivalry) and an individual cannot be prevented from consuming the good whether or not the individual pays for it (non-excludability). Public goods result in *market failure* where the *free market economy* does not produce results that are both necessary and efficient for the economy a whole. As Joseph Stiglitz (1999a) argues: 'The central public policy implication of public goods is that the state must play some role in the provision of such goods; otherwise they will be undersupplied' (p. 311). Stiglitz combines two concepts that have developed over the last couple of decades: 'the concept of global public goods and the notion of knowledge as a global public good' (p. 308). In 'Public Policy for A Knowledge Economy' Stiglitz (1999b) indicates:

> Knowledge is different from other goods: it has many of the central properties of a public good, indeed of a global public good. While government has a key role in protecting all property rights, its role in intellectual property rights is far more complicated: the appropriate definition of these rights is not even obvious. And in the knowledge economy, the dangers of a monopolization are perhaps even greater than in industrial economies.

Simon Marginson (2008) argues 'Global information flows in the fast growing 'open source' knowledge system are providing the conditions for the evolution of a larger and more active *global public sphere*' and he goes on to suggest 'like global information flows in general, the global public sphere partly breaks open the controls that national governments have traditionally exercised in relation to the flows of knowledge accessed by their citizens. It also elevates, alongside the state and the market, a third set of agencies that are wholly reducible to neither.' Gert Verschraegen and Michael Schiltz (2007) in "Knowledge as a Global Public

Good: The Role and Importance of Open Access" argue for the provision of knowledge as a global public good through OS and OA:

By doing away with technological, legal and monetary barriers to knowledge, the Open Access movement has created unprecedented possibilities to treat knowledge and science as global public goods, the benefits of which reach across borders and population groups. The OA and OS movements a play a crucial role in the emergence of a truly 'global public', which is principally unbound and not limited by spatial forms of integration of society.32 In the OA model, knowledge is public, non-exclusive and available for all to enjoy (p. 163).

They claim that OA thereby actualizes knowledge's inherent potential to be a universal good with non-excludable benefits and that scientific knowledge qualifies for being globally public, because it does not discriminate between users.

SECTION II: THE FUTURE

FROM LEARNED SOCIETIES TO LEARNING SOCIETIES

Globalization leads to cultural changes including the influences that shape and condition the learning society. According to Schein (1985), there are three levels that exist in culture: basic assumptions, values, and artifacts. These assumptions may be adapted as interpretative schemes for individuals to react to ongoing surrounding activities, interactive relationships, and even collective actions (Van Maanen & Barley, 1985). Globalization and the knowledge economy concerns the promotion of the learning society, the culture and value of emphasizing knowledge production and cross boundaries of cooperation.

There are different types of learning society in the literature and policies that emphasize the transformation to the learning society seems (e.g. Faure et al., 1972; Husein, 1986; EC, 1996; NCIHE, 1997; Su, 2007). Sometimes transformation to a learning society is recognized as more of developed countries' policies (Bartlett et al., 2000). In fact, the concept of the learning society is also justified by the purposes of economic strength and civic cohesion (Coffield, 1997a). Such a discourse reveals that the learning society is envisaged as a carrier, or a facilitator, for something other than itself; it becomes a facilitator of economic progress, or a structure which enables civic power to be relayed (Su, 2007) and involves an informational paradigm of development. Coffield (1997b) states learning society may be viewed as 'an economized civic society', a society planned to 'ensure social integration as well as economic success' (pp. 450).

The concept of the learning economy was first coined and has been championed by Bengt-Åke Lundvall, a Swedish economist from Aalborg University, who uses the term to talk about a new context for European innovation policy.[6] Lundvall (1994, 2003) first used the concept in the mid 1990s in a series of working papers to discuss technological change, innovation and institutional learning directly applying it to the learning society and economy, to universities, and to education more generally in the 2000s, culminating in *How Europe's Economies Learn* (Lorenz & Lundvall, 2006) that focuses on diversity in European competence building systems, organization, labour markets and corporate governance and the links between education and science-industry. The concept and theory of the learning economy is a refinement of the 'knowledge economy' concept based on the way a set of interlocking forces (ecologies) in information/knowledge intensities, distributed new social media, and greater computer networking and connectivity have contributed to the heightened significance of human capital formations, mode of social production and an emphasis on learning processes (Peters, 2010).

We believe that the concept of the learned society provides a complementary global civic model for development especially given arguments concerning science as a global public good based upon freely accessible scientific knowledge in peer reviewed and governed open journal systems.

JOURNAL KNOWLEDGE PRODUCTION

Henry Oldenburg and his colleagues claimed the basic functions of journals at the Royal Society in 1664–65 are registration, dissemination, certification and archiving. These functions are still the dominant ones over 400 years later (Mabe, 2010; McCartan, 2010). McCartan (2010) states: "…that there was no reason to challenge the role of journals in asserting the ownership of an idea, attracting recognition, establishing reputation and reward, and leaving a permanent record." (p. 238)

Phillips (2009) claims that the journals industry operates with a settled business model which has stable and durable relationships among publishers, scholars, libraries and agents. This journal knowledge production serves as a form of knowledge production however it is different from the production of other kinds of goods in a market. The journal knowledge production can be viewed as an *information good.* Quah (2003) distinguishes information goods from ordinary ones in a number of ways. First, they are *nonrival,* that means their usage by one consumer does not prevent corresponding use by any number of other consumers. Secondly, they are *infinitely expansible,* therefore their quantity can be increased arbitrarily with little or none cost. Thirdly, they are *aspatial,* meaning any copy is the original and is possible to be everywhere at the same time. These characters make it possible for journals which adapting internet to provide to different and great numbers of consumers simultaneously. Peters (2009) also states that one of the important features of information goods is that knowledge is often classified as a public good. Academic journals are responsible to reward academic innovation and spread to the society. Quah (2003) claims the intellectual property rights emerged to react to the tension between individual rewards and public disseminations.

In addition, competing journals are different from competing markets where substitutions of each other occur (Berstrom and Bergstrom, 2006). These journals complementally publishing relates with one and other. Articles may be similar to previous studies in some aspects but not in substitutable ways. Knowledge is added through this process of studies built upon previous studies or relevant studies published in the form of articles. McCartan (2010) states the transforming business model "reader pays" subscription to "author pays, open access" one in recent decades increases efficiency. "Author pays, open access" is one form that the enormous potential gains from the Internet which changes the form of excluding potential readers toward open access.

In addition, Peer-to-Peer (P2P) is an important feature of globalization and journal knowledge production. One of the traditional relationships among scholars is the P2P element. The peer reviews and interaction encourage the knowledge production and quality. P2P also further develop into peer production relationships. This peer production involves the cross boundaries and encourages collective contributions. Globalization often makes the cross boundaries more internationalized to include more researchers cooperation.

GLOBAL LEARNING AND KNOWLEDGE CREATION

Global learning is a feature of the contemporary learning society. There different forms of globalization (Torrs, 2009) which also influence different form of learning society. In relevant literature and policies learning society is considered as purpose-oriented directive which is top-down approach (Su, 2007). Howard (1990, also in Su, 2007) explains this kind of approach set group-level requirements for each individual to meet these requirement as necessary for learning. This top-down approach clearly put learning activities to achieve goals that above individual level to social expectations involving economic or civil needs (Raven, 2005; Welton, 2005; Su, 2007). Su (2007) claims this top-down form learning society deal with the what individuals should learn by meeting with pre-given goals. However, the individual learning in present has changed toward more of personal concerns.

The collective learning in learning society depends on the interactive relationship of individuals in the society. This bottom-up learning society does not set pre-given learning aims based on particular social perspectives of what to learn, but based on individual's subjectivity.

> Three aspects that characterize the practices of the bottom-up learning society:/lifelong learning, the individualization of learning, and learning beyond education, which are outlined respectively in the subsequent subsections/serve as the context for understanding what is meant by the learning society as itself (Su, 2007).

Smart (1992) claims what we learn becomes temporary form due to the fast changing character of modern time. This kind of rapid changes in present era makes the framework of our learning problematic and comes to the age Barnett (1997) describes as 'supercomplexity'. The fast changing framework also leads to the uncertainty concerns to the world where Lyotard (1984) claims as sensing the incredulity to the traditional legitimacy of certainty, trustable metanarratives. The ideas and discourses have shortened lives which may be replaced. Scott (1997) claims that only ephemeral "discourses" may bloom. As discourses are no longer stable and trustworthy as traditional metanarratives, they may be changed or reconstructed frequently in modern era. Su (2007) claims due to this temporary truth of discourses, it is needed to relearn new discourses through time. The life long learning becomes quite important for individual to learn new things or understand the changes of discourses in present society. The form of knowledge learning and producing also change with the technology develops.

Edwards (2001, also in Su, 2007) claims: "modularization, open learning and the increasing use of information and communications technologies, for example, seek to extend the range of choice available to learners and provide the means for charting routes that meet their individual needs, interests and circumstances" (p. 40). Technology empowers individuals' learning by providing cross boundaries interaction and freedom of access. These technology improvements make it possible for individuals to learn based on their differences. Individuals can interact and build upon other information to participate in knowledge learning and production. The learning society based on the individualizing of education learning can be viewed as similar as educated society or education centered society (Su, 2007). In such learning society, individuals entertain themselves through learning activities by pursuit truth and solving problems (Su, 2007).

The character of technology as individualized learning society that individuals integrate knowledge by themselves defers from previous 'top-down' form which provides formation ahead (Su, 2007). Tough (1979) states while learning society focuses on economic progress and developing citizenship may result in missing the individual's self automatic learning based on their own willingness and purposes.

> Bottom-up, endogenous growth, based on the strength of learning individuals' mobility, constitutes the microprocess that occurs in the learning lifeworld. The sharing and diffusion of information and knowledge among individuals constitute the process of decentralized and unintended development, based largely on the spontaneity of individuals' efforts and deliberation, while the development of the economy and citizenship for society as a whole is perceived by individuals not as aims but the conditions that allow their learning to be sustained (Su, 2007: 202).

Learning network is more than just variety of collection of individuals cross space with different resource but connecting with each other (Su, 2007). Su (2007) claims that using network as metaphor (Jones, 2004) dose not directly refer to new technologies even thought these technologies can be main tools to make the links. This network does not mean computer networks, but more of the interactive, decentralize, flexible and non hierarchical character relationship (Harris, 2000). Through networking process, each individual achieve vary of learning aims without having to follow some hierarchical directions to singular perspectives or actable learning outcome creating multiple representations (Su, 2007).

> By networking, individuals in the learning society learn effectively, in terms of the learning resources and opportunities which are distributed, and extend their availability so that individuals know where to find the people and resources with which they want to be in contact (Su, 2007).

Collective learning is also another feature for learning society. All individuals can contribute by sharing information and knowledge through interactive networking. Each one can learn through the interactive discussions with others as learning by peers. In fact, this P2P relationship also represents the feature collective learning and knowledge production (Bauwens, 2010).

> It is the ongoing effect rooted in individuals' willingness to share their thoughts on what they learn, making it possible for others to collaborate with them in action. Through the pursuit of individuals' own needs and interests, discoveries are made and uploaded into the area of public knowledge for the benefit of everyone (Su, 2007).

Interactions between individuals in learning process are a kind of social capital in learning society. Communication technologies improvements make it easier for individuals to approach learning resources. However, there is some questions about equity issues that only those who have capital of using these technologies are benefits. In other words, some disadvantage people are missing their learning opportunities in learning society. Individuals are categorized in a different way, based 'not on wealth and property but on the distribution of knowledge and skill' (Young, 1998, p. 141). While the disadvantaged and underprivileged feel excluded and wonder 'whose learning society?' (Macrae et al., 1997, p. 499), the privileged have their own anxieties about preventing themselves from being trapped or overwhelmed by the unprecedented speed of change and growth of information (Su, 2007).

SCHOLARSHIP IN THE DIGITAL AGE

Digital scholarship can be published quickly, which allows a scholar to disseminate promptly the results of their research and readers to gain ready access to information for use in their classrooms or research (Purdy & Walker, 2010). Digital scholarship requires authors to create texts that are publishable and readable online. Scholarship and scholarly communication is changing with individuals being able to unleash their creativity. These practices by faculty will extend slowly to cultural changes at the disciplinary level and ultimately to new interdisciplinary standards that are expressed by institutions when deciding tenure and promotion practices. For some considerable time, higher education institutions have overlooked an opportunity to support innovative and creative faculty. Faculty members have been exploring ways in which works of authorship in the new digital medium with the hopes it can enhance teaching and learning within the new forms of scholarship. These innovations are essential in keeping scholarship vital and effective, and be supported. Encouraging these innovations in teaching and scholarship reaches to the core mission and values of our institutions (Lynch, 2003).

Many academic discussions often argue that the most important selling point for a turn toward digital learning environments is the format of texts. While this may be productive, the discussions tend to focus on improving the ease and minimizing the expense of bringing information to readers. This limits the value of digital publications to practical aspects of delivery and framing publishing digital scholarship as a material delivery choice rather than a knowledge-making practice. In doing so, what is ignored are the benefits and the advancement of nonlinear thinking which in turn allows for the possibility of exploration and design. New technologies have influenced tenure and promotion considerations. Technology provides new venues of publication and is creating what scholarly activity and production means. These technologies include knowledge products and new approaches to knowledge construction. It has been difficult for faculty committees to categorize the scholarly value of digital work, as faculty members continue to use and create digital scholarship tools (Purdy & Walker, 2010).

The situation is even worse for faculty members who are concerned not just with distribution opportunities, but how to use the digital medium for new works of authorship. Faculty have been forced to take upon themselves the problem of arguing the legitimacy of investing their time in works of digital scholarship and others who are making comparisons to the traditional scholarly publishing outlets. This is a problem that academe must deal with among the disciplines, faculty committees, and institutions. In the world of electronic distribution of journal articles, the concept of "the journal" becomes subjective. This terminology is required to still fit itself into traditional academic outlets. Instead of being directed by outside constraints of defining forms of knowledge, institutions must take back the knowledge that they produce. Universities already have the capacity and the infrastructure necessary for archiving their faculty's contribution to the academy (Cleary, 2007).

PEER REVIEW AND PEER LEARNING

Digital scholarship connects scholarly research to students and the public in nontraditional ways. The authors present research in a digital form, which may include links to primary source material and teaching guides. In this format, design and accessibility are important, and unfortunately, those quick to dismiss all digital work as teaching or outreach can overlook the research element. The confusion over what digital scholarship is and how to evaluate it can affect promotion and tenure decisions in academic institutions. The growth of internet technology has changed the way researchers convey and access scholarship. Although some academic departments are supportive of researchers who have done digital scholarship, many still do not acknowledge that scholarship can be produced in a digital format. The problem lies largely with the lack of respected peer review for digital scholarship. Those who are not involved with producing digital scholarship are often completely unaware of the effort and research that goes into these projects. This places an undue burden on individuals who not only perform the original scholarship but also must build a case for the work's value when presenting them for tenure. There is a critical need for a system of peer review in which the academic value of a work of digital scholarship is universally accepted by the faculty within a discipline. Only at this level will the risk of producing digital scholarship be elevated for the scholar not only for gaining tenure, but also for acknowledgement throughout the academy (Cross, 2008).

It is common practice for peers to review journal articles and to tutor in tertiary educational programs, although disparity exists surrounding its origins. Perfecting knowledge for the purpose of sharing through accurate communication is the goal of the peer review process that has been created and maintained by cooperative societies and commercial publishers. Peer review necessitates a speedy review by a motivated reviewing committee. The peer committee must have respect for the intellectual freedom of authors. Peer committees must have respect for author ownership of ideas experts capable of reviewing manuscripts should not have interests that would allow for plagiarism or even preemptive presentation of the author's ideas. Post publication peer review should lead to links for retractions by authors or convincing proof of false conclusions of archived published papers. Removal of papers with false conclusions, even when requested by the author, is an ethical violation against the record of imperfect truth, which has a function in assisting the endeavor of researchers in not repeating the errors of their colleagues (Cleary, 2007).

The collaboration encouraged by digital scholarship extends beyond coauthors producing texts. Digital scholarship fosters more collaboration among readers, writers, and textual sources. Digital texts promote a culture of sharing as they can be circulated easily among many people, for example, through social bookmarking sites, email, and discussion boards (Purdy & Walker, 2010). Peer learning is one method to encourage meaningful learning, which involves students teaching and learning from each other. It involves a sharing of ideas, knowledge and experiences and emphasizes interdependent as opposed to independent learning (Boud, 2001). Peer learning is a "two-way reciprocal learning activity" (Boud et al., 2001, 3) in which there is mutual benefit to the parties involved. The reciprocal nature of the activity is key as students do not hold power over each other by virtue of their position or responsibilities (Topping, 2005).

Peer learning can be both informal and formal. Informal peer learning occurs implicitly when students discuss lectures, assignments, projects and exams in casual social settings. A major benefit of peer learning is that it promotes a transferable skill that students can apply to other courses and real-world professional settings. Peer learning also promotes lifelong learning and is linked to generic capabilities of teamwork and interpersonal skills that employers view highly (Tan, 2003). On the other hand, peer learning is not without its challenges, as lecturers need to consider the context in which it is introduced, the general goals and learning outcomes, the congruence between the peer learning strategies and assessment tasks, and the preparation of both staff and students for the initiative (Topping, 2005).

OPENNESS: CONCEPTS AND COPYRIGHT

The concept of openness in education practices means different things to different scholars and institutions. Lewis and Spencer (1986, 9–10) described openness in education as the adoption of measures to encourage widespread access to and participation in education. Openness and transformation in education could also mean what choices are given to the learner in any system of education. Sometimes, the choices that learners have are circumscribed by physical barriers such as time, space and the pace at which learning may be undertaken. Individual and social constraints such as age, gender, and ethnicity and class structures complicate the notions of openness and transformation of education, especially when related to issues of access. The degree of flexibility or inflexibility of education programs can also frustrate or promote openness. Openness admits that education and learning have traditionally been closed by various barriers such as entrance requirements, time constraints, financial demands or geographical distances (Vambe, 2005).

"Openness has become a leading source of innovation in the world global digital economy, increasingly adopted by world governments, international agencies, and multinationals, as well as by leading educational institutions as a means of promoting scientific inquiry and international collaboration" (Peters, Marginson, & Murphy, 2009, 203). Openness can be a major driving force to knowledge creation and social and economic advancement through the development of a knowledge society. Openness is increasingly receiving high degrees of attention from scholars, professionals and policy makers in recent years. A growing number of publications and conferences are exploring these subjects from various angles. Openness is becoming essential to ideas in the growing area of policy development in higher education.

As institutions of higher education try to resolve their own funding issues with the rising costs of technology, some institutions are turning to open source software. Open source technology users point to an extensive body of research that explores the benefits and risks of open source in the context of social movement theory and appeals to the common good. In doing so, institutions have been quick to research and adopt open source software for the development of instructional content and delivery systems. A well-known example is MIT's Open Course Ware Web site. This is an example of free access to instructional materials to be used by anyone. The materials are targeted to educators and learners with use being the enhancement of personal knowledge.

The information age advanced the value of intellectual property as a critical commodity in society. The rise of the Internet and its global adoption in libraries around the world has created countless legal problems. While this new communications medium offers tremendous capacity for improving society and the lives of ordinary citizens, it is only natural that legal problems from the analog world would arise along with brand new ones. Many people have questioned whether the old laws and legal traditions will survive the changes wrought by the Internet. It is indeed appealing to think that society might be completely restructured so that law plays a less important role. This is unlikely to be the case, however. Society developed laws and the legal system to assist in settling disputes, and there are already significant disputes that have arisen in the electronic world (Gasaway, 1998).

Intellectual property refers to creations of the mind such as inventions, literary and artistic works, symbols, names, images and designs used in commerce and en)compasses copyrights, trademarks and patents. The term intellectual property describes the creator's legal rights and not the intellectual work itself. Copyright laws, like most intellectual property protections, vary by country. Although copyright is implicit, the author must register that copyright before fi ling a copyright infringement lawsuit. The term of copyright protection is generally considered the life of the author plus 70 years. Copyright protection is subject to certain limitations, most notably the doctrine of fair use (Section 107 of the Act), which protects such areas as teaching, scholarship and news reporting, as well as the public domain (Bonifield and Tomas, 2009).

Preservation of scholarly works is an essential prerequisite to any claims to digital scholarly legitimacy for authoring in the new medium; without being able to claim such works are a permanent part of the scholarly record, it's very hard to argue that they not only deserve but demand full consideration as contributions to scholarship. Most individual faculty lack the time, resources, or expertise to ensure preservation of their own scholarly work even in the short term, and clearly can't do it in the long term that extends beyond their careers; the long term can only be addressed by an organizationally based strategy. The revolution in scholarly communications is not limited to the development of new genres of scholarly works that are enabled by the digital medium; even traditional forms such as journal articles now frequently include supplementary datasets and analysis tools. Scholarship has become data intensive; it is supported and documented by data and tools that complement interpretive works of authorship (Lynch, 2003).

CONCLUSION

The learned society provides a model that is neither state nor market that has a long history of a commitment to public knowledge and science based on peer review and governance as an essential characteristic of science and scholarship, along with replicability, testability and the cultivation of a critical attitude. Learned societies also provide a useful set of norms upon which to generalize and establish the learning society as a generalized science model committed to the public good. In the digital age new Web 2.0 technologies provide new ways of enhancing and building upon peer production of knowledge. The Internet has become the foundational cyberinfrastructure that facilitates scholarly communication and deep data-sharing and archiving affecting every stage of the scholarly production and transforming the historical concepts that historically comprised the legal and economic architecture that grew up around intellectual property rights. Mass digitization of books, electronic books and new forms of open journals systems have greatly expanded the availability of scholarly publication and scientific data changing both the logics of production and consumption (reception) of academic texts. New models of open science and open knowledge production based on principles of global public goods and an ethos of sharing and collaboration create new transnational academic communities in global knowledge ecologies that intersect in novel ways.

Digital scholarship connects scholarly research to students and the public in nontraditional ways. Authors present research in a digital form, which may include links to primary source material and teaching guides. In this format, design and accessibility are important, and, unfortunately, those quick to dismiss all digital work as teaching or outreach can overlook the research element. The confusion over what digital scholarship is and how to evaluate it can affect promotion and tenure decisions in academic institutions. Mechanisms for peer review must be created by scholarly associations and applied to digital scholarship to ensure this form of scholarship is acknowledged and rewarded. It is in this context that we would suggest that learned societies today need to reposition themselves in order to expand their contribution to public science and education by exploring the new possibilities for knowledge creation and distribution of the peer production of knowledge enabled by a range of Web technologies and social media.

NOTES

[1] See http://www.scholarly-societies.org/

[2] With the following geographical distribution as of January 2003: International 16.4%, North America 23.3% (including USA 15.4%), South America 4.3%, Oceania 3.7%, Europe 32.7%, Asia 10.5%, Africa 1.9%

[3] See Easton, Stewart C., *Roger Bacon and His Search for a Universal Science* (New York: Columbia University Press, 1952).

[4] For a brief popular history of secret societies see Barrett (2007).

[5] http://www.npg.org.uk/collections/search/portrait.php?firstRun=true&sText=Frontispiece+to+The+ History+of+the+Royal%2DSociety+of+London+%281667%29+by+Thomas+Sprat+&search=sp&r No=0.

[6] For Lundvall's publications see his webpage at http://www.business.aau.dk/ike/members/bal.html.

REFERENCES

Bauwens, M. (2010). Toward a P2P Economy, in D. Araya & M.A. Peters (Eds.), Education in the creative economy: Knowledge and learning in the age of innovation (pp. 305–330). New York: NY: Peter Lang.

Bonifield, C.M. & Tomas, A.M. (2009). "Intellectual property issues for marketers in the virtual world," *Brand Management, 16*(8): 571–581.

Boud, D. (2001). "Introduction: making the move to peer learning," in: D. Boud, R. Cohen & J. Sampson (Eds.) *Peer learning in higher education.* London: Kogan Page, 1–19.

Boud, D., Cohen, R. & Sampson, J. (2001). "Peer learning and assessment," in: D. Boud, R. Cohen, & J. Sampson (Eds.) *Peer learning in higher education.* London: Kogan Page, 67–81.

Cleary, Daniel E. (2007). "Incentives for Deconstruction of the E-Journal," *The Acquisitions Librarian, 19*(1): 135–144.

Coffield, F. (1997b). Introduction and Overview: Attempts to Reclaim the Concept of the Learning Society, *Journal of Education Policy,* vol. 12, no. 6, pp. 449–455.

Cook, Alan (1997). "Essay review: Seeds of the scientific revolution" *Notes Rec. R. Soc. Lond. 51,* 327–334.

Cross, J. G. (2008). Reviewing digital scholarship: The need for discipline-based peer review, *Journal of Web Librarianship, 2*(4), 549–566.

Dalrymple, Dana (2003). "Scientific Knowledge as a Global Public Good: Contributions to Innovation and the Economy". In: The Role of Scientific and Technical Data and Information in the Public Domain: Proceedings of a Symposium (2003). Board on International Scientific Organizations (BISO), at http://www.nap.edu/openbook.php?record_id=10785&page=35.

Eamon, William (1985). "From the Secrets of Nature to Public Knowledge: The Origins of the Concept of Openness in Science," *Minerva, 23*(3): 321–347.

Fara, Patricia (2003). "The first President of the Royal Society," *Endeavour, 27*(4): 148–149.

Fischer, Kuno (1857). *Francis Bacon of Verulam: Realistic Philosophy and Its Age,* trans. John Oxenford. London: Longman, Brown, Green, Longmans, & Roberts.

Gasaway, L.N. (1998). "Copyright, the internet, and other legal issues," *Journal of the American Society for Information Science, 49*(11): 1003–1009.

Henry, John (1999). "Magic and the Origins of Modern Science," *The Lancet,* 354.

Henry, John (2002). *The Scientific Revolution and the Origins of Modern Science.* 2nd Edt, New York Palgrave.

Henry, John (2002b). *Knowledge is Power: How Magic, the Government and an Apocalyptic Vision Inspired Francis Bacon to Create Modern Science.* Cambridge: Icon Books.

Howard, R. (1990). Introduction, in: R. Howard (Ed.) *The learning imperative.* Boston: Harvard Business School.

Jones, C. (2004). Networks and learning: communities, practices and the metaphor of networks, *ALT-J, 12*(1), 81–93.

Kassall, Lauran (2011). "Secrets Revealed: Alchemical Books in Early-Modern England" *History of Science, 49*(1): 61–87.

Lewis, R. & Spencer, D. (1986). *What is open learning?* London, Council for Educational Technology.

Lynch, C. A. (2003). Institutional Repositories: Essential Infrastructure for Scholarship in the Digital Age. *ARL, 226,* 1–7.

Lynch, William T. (2001). *Solomon's Child: Method in the Early Royal Society of London.* Stanford, CA: Stanford University Press.

Lynch, William, T. (2005). "A Society of Baconians? The Collective Development of Bacon's Method in the Rpyal Society of London". In: Solomon, Julie Robin & Martin, Catherine Gimelli (2005). (Eds.) *Francis Bacon and the Refiguring of Early Modern Thought: Essays to Commemorate The Advancement of Learning* (1605–2005). pp. 173–202. Aldershot: Ashgate.

Lyotard, J.F. (1984). *The postmodern condition: A report on knowledge,* G. Bennington & B. Massumi (Trans.). Manchester, UK: Manchester University Press.

Marginson, Simon (2008). "The knowledge economy and the potentials of the global public sphere". Paper presented at the Beijing Forum, at http://www.universityworldnews.com/filemgmt_data/files/Beijing%20Forum%202008%20Simon%20Marginson.pdf.

McCartan, P. (2010). Journals and the Production of knowledge: A publishing perspective. British Journal of Political Science. 40, p. 237–248.

McClellan, James E. III. (2002). "Learned Societies", Alan Charles Kors, ed., *Oxford Encyclopedia of the Enlightenment.* New York: Oxford University Press.

McCarton, P. (2010). Journals and the Production of Knowledge: A Publishing Perspective, *British journal of political science,* 40, 237–248.

Ornstein, M. (1963). The role of scientific societies in the seventeenth century. 3rd edn. Hamden: Archon Books.

Peters, M., Marginson, S. & Murphy, P. (2009). *Creativity and the global knowledge economy.* New York: Peter Lang.

Powell, J., (1886). In: *Testimony Before the Joint Commission* (letter to W. B. Allison,February 26, 1886), 1082.

Porter, R. (2003). *The Cambridge History of Science: Eighteenth-Century science.*

Porter, R., Park, K. & Daston, L. (2006). *The Cambridge History of Science: Early modern science.* Cambridge: Cambridge University Press.

Purdy, J.P. & Walker, J.R. (2010). "Valuing digital scholarship: Exploring the changing realities of intellectual work." *The Modern Language Association of America: 177–195.*

Quah, D., (2003). Digital Goods and the New Economy, *CEPR Discussion Papers*, 3846, Retrieved from: http://ideas.repec.org/p/cpr/ceprdp/3846.html

Samuelson, Paul A. (1954). "The Pure Theory of Public Expenditure," *Review of Economics and Statistics* (The MIT Press) *36*(4): 387–389.

Smart, B. (1992). Modern conditions, postmodern controversies. London: Routledge.

Sprat, Thomas (1667]1958) *History of the Royal Society.* St. Louis, MO: Washington University Press.

Stiglitz, Joseph E. (1999). Knowledge as a Global Public Good. In: Inge Kaul, Isabelle Grunberg and Marc A. Stern (Eds.) *Global Public Goods International Cooperation in the 21st Century.* New York: Oxford University Press.

Stiglitz, Joseph E. (1999). "Public Policy for a Knowledge Economy." At 10.1.1.123.9173.

Su, Y.H. (2007). The learning society as itself: lifelong learning, individualization of learning, and beyond education, *Studies in Continuing Education, 29*(2), pp. 195–206.

Tan, O.S. (2003). *Problem-based learning innovation: Using problems to power learning in the 21st century.* Singapore: Thomas learning.

Topping, K. (2008). "Peer-assisted learning: A planning and implementation framework. Guide Supplement 30.1—Viewpoint," *Medical Teacher, 30,* 440–445.

Torres, C.A., (2009). *Education and neoliberal globalization.* New York, NY: Routledge.

Tough, A. M. (1979). *The adult's learning projects: a fresh approach to theory and practice in adult learning.* Toronto: Ontario Institute for Studies in Education.

Turner, Stephen (2008). The Social Study of Science before Kuhn. *The Handbook of Science and Technology Studies,* edited by Edward J. Hackett, Olga Amsterdamska, Michael Lynch, & Judy Wajcman. Cambridge, MA: MIT Press, pp. 33–62.

Vambe, M.T. (2005). "Opening and transforming South African education," *Open Learning 20*(3): 285–293.

Verschraegen, Gert & Schiltz, Michael (2007). in "Knowledge as a Global Public Good: The Role and Importance of Open Access," Societies without Borders, *2*(2): 157–174.

Weinberger, J. (1985). "Science, Faith, and Politics: Francis Bacon and the Utopian Roots of the Modern Age: A Commentary of Bacon's *Advancement of Learning.*" Ithaca: Cornell University Press.

Printed in the United States
By Bookmasters